IMPROVING YOUR SPELLING
Third Edition

Falk S. Johnson

University of Illinois
at Chicago Circle

HOLT, RINEHART AND WINSTON

New York · Chicago · San Francisco · Atlanta ·
Dallas · Montreal · Toronto

First published as A *Spelling Guide
and Workbook* in 1959; a second
edition, *A Self-Improvement Guide to
Spelling,* was published in 1965.
This edition includes some materials
originally published by Houghton
Mifflin Company in Falk S. Johnson's
Improving What You Write (1965). The
author is grateful for permission to use
those materials here.

Library of Congress Cataloging in Publication Data

Johnson, Falk S.
  Improving Your Spelling
  Second ed. published in 1965 under title:
A self-improvement guide to spelling.
  1. Spellers. I. Title.
PE1145.2.J6 1979   428'.1   78-11942
ISBN 0-03-043031-3

Printed in the United States of America
1 2 3   059   9 8 7 6 5 4

CONTENTS

IMPROVING
YOUR SPELLING

TO THE TEACHER

This book, like its earlier editions, is the result of an attempt to answe two questions:

1. Which words do college students most often misspell?

2. What causes those particular misspellings?

The answer to the first question (which words?) was sought by consulting almost a dozen lists of words previously recorded as most frequently misspelled, especially in college but also in high school. Those lists were consolidated into a single composite list, which is included as Appendix F in this volume.

The answer to the second question (what caused those misspellings?) was sought by analyzing every word in the composite list, searching for the probable reason for each misspelling. Each of the causes, thus discovered, is the subject of a chapter in this book. That search for causes also led to the general conclusion that the underlying problems in spelling are of two fundamentally different kinds: personal and verbal.

Personal problems are to be found in the person trying to spell, not in the word that he or she is trying to spell. Typical of personal problems affecting spelling are poor vision, a foreign background, and just plain carelessness or irresponsibility. In contrast, verbal problems are found, not in the person, but in the word itself. They are largely the result of the inconsistent ways in which letters are combined to form words. For instance, why is *pneumonia* spelled with a *p*? And why isn't *through* spelled *thru*? Such illogical combinations of letters are the chief cause of verbal problems.

This book is unique in that it deals with both kinds of problems, the personal as well as the verbal. In addition, it provides diagnostic aids so that students may quickly discover which problems are (and are not) causing them trouble in spelling. Guided by these diagnostic aids, students can concentrate their efforts on the problems which they have and, just as important, ignore the problems which they do not have.

In more detail, this book provides two sets of diagnostic aids: one set for students working alone, and the other set for students participating in a class. If working alone, students take (and grade) the pretest at the beginning of each chapter, but they study only the chapters where the pretest reveals a need for instruction. Students in a class may also do that. Or for them and their teacher to get more quickly a panoramic view of all their verbal problems in spelling, they may take the diagnostic test in Appendix A. Appendix B, "Interpreting the Test," enables them to compare their performance on the test with that of earlier students; Appendix C, "Planning Your Program," shows which chapters they should concentrate on (or ignore) as they seek to solve their own individual problems. Appendix D, "Final Test," may be used after instruction—either individualized or in class—has been completed. It deals with the same problems that were covered in the diagnostic test, but its words are, for the most part, different from those in the earlier test

The author believes that more misspellings are caused by personal than by verbal problems. That is why the chapters concerned with personal problems have been placed first, in Part One. It is recommended that all users of the book, whether working alone or in a group, take the pretests for these four chapters and, where the pretests show a need, study these chapters. Individuals working alone may than proceed through the rest of the book a chapter at a time, but students in a class may, if the teacher desires, take the diagnostic test (Appendix A) at this point to get a quick preview of the verbal problems that each student will need to concentrate on in later portions of the book. Of course this preview will also enable the teacher to plan in advance the work which the class as a whole most needs before the unit on spelling is completed.

Chapters 5–17 deal one by one with the chief verbal causes of misspellings as revealed by the composite list (Appendix F). These chapters are arranged according to the total number of misspellings attributable, in one of the underlying lists, to each cause. For example, unstressed vowels (Chapter 5) led to more than four thousand misspellings in this list, while internal doubling (Chapter 17) led to little more than a hundred. As a result of this arrangement, students are likely to work first with the problems causing them the most trouble, last with those causing the least.

The final two chapters, 18 and 19, deal with problems in spelling that were not discernible in the lists but are still too important to be ignored in a guide to spelling: the problems of competing spellings (*favor* or *favour?*) and of compound words (why *postmaster* but *post office?*).

In brief, this book attempts to provide teachers with what they need for helping college students to achieve the greatest improvement in spelling with the least expenditure of effort on the part of both the teacher and the student. Just as earlier editions have helped thousands to do this, so, it is hoped, will this edition help others.

When the author used an earlier edition in class, it brought about marked improvement in the spelling of many students. That fact was demonstrated by a comparison of the performance of students on the diagnostic test, taken before instruction, and on the final test, taken after instruction. Of course you yourself may make such a comparison with your own students, if you wish.

The earlier comparison showed, in the first place, that the book can decrease markedly the number of words misspelled by most students. On an average, that number was cut in half. Because the two tests deal with the same problems in spelling but, with few exceptions, consist of different individual words, the performance of students on the two tests showed improvement, not merely in the spelling of a limited number of individual words, but, more significantly, in the ability to solve the most common problems in spelling—problems affecting the spelling of multitudes of words.

Perhaps just as important, the comparison also showed a substantial increase in the tendency of students to consult their dictionary for the spellings of the very words that they miss. On both tests the students were asked to mark as "doubtful" all words they were not sure how to spell correctly. On the first test most of the missed words were not marked as "doubtful"—an indication that a dictionary would not have been consulted even if it had been available. On the second test, however, most of the missed words were marked as "doubtful" by many students—an indication that they would have consulted a dictionary if it had been available. Indeed, a few students marked as "doubtful" all the words missed on the second test, while no students did that on the first.

The actual improvement brought about by the earlier editions should therefore be measured, not only by the decreased number of misspellings, but also by the increased skill in solving the most common problems in spelling and, perhaps most important, by the increased tendency of students to consult a dictionary for spellings.

It is hoped that this new edition, which has been extensively revised, will bring about even more improvement in spelling than the earlier editions did.

TO THE STUDENT

You want to improve your spelling because you know that poor spelling can hurt you. It can keep you from achieving top grades in school and from gaining professional advancement in the years beyond school. It can also damage you socially, both now and later. In brief, poor spelling can hold you back in many important ways throughout your entire life.

This book, which can help you to improve your spelling, has been designed for use in either of two ways: as a textbook in an organized class or as a self-improvement book for you to work with alone. If it is used in a class, your teacher will make the assignments and will give you a schedule for completing them. On the other hand, if you work with it alone, you may move through it at the speed most convenient for you—fast if you work intensively and steadily or more slowly if you must spread out your work over a longer period of time. Regardless of how you use this book, it can, with your help, improve your spelling.

You may work with it alone because it has been designed so that you will not need somebody to dictate words for you to spell. Also you will not have to wait for somebody to grade your spellings. That is because all questions are in the form of blanks for you to fill in, and all answers are on nearby pages so that you can instantly check your own work. For those reasons you can improve your spelling at the speed that best suits you—quickly if possible but more slowly if necessary.

The plan for using the book is simple. At the beginning of each chapter is a brief pretest which you should take and grade—a process requiring, perhaps, a couple of minutes. If you make no mistakes on the pretest, you may skip the chapter and move on to the next pretest. On the other hand, if you miss a part of the pretest, you should study the accompanying chapter, do the exercise following it, and finally take a posttest on the material covered by the chapter. In that way you may move through the book, studying some chapters carefully while skipping others. How many chapters you study and how many you skip will be determined by how many different problems in spelling you have—few or many. The pretests themselves will show you which problems you have and which you do not have.

Earlier editions of this book have helped thousands of students to improve their spelling. In the same way, this new edition can help you. Use it.

PART I GENERAL AIDS FOR SPELLING

Sometimes spelling can be improved quickly. The most powerful aids, capable of bringing about the greatest improvement with the least study, are presented in the next four chapters. The first chapter, "Proofreading," can enable you to search out your own misspellings better than ever before. The second, "A Sense of Doubt," can increase your use of a dictionary and therefore decrease your misspellings. The third, "Consultation with Specialists," can help you to overcome certain handicaps that may, unknown to you, be hurting your spelling—for instance, a handicap in seeing. And the fourth, "Personalized List of Misspellings," can make your further study of spelling more efficient by limiting it to the words that you actually misspell.

1

PROOFREADING: THE SEARCH FOR MISSPELLINGS

PRETEST 1

Part One
Underline the misspelled words in this paragraph:

> This morning an accident occurred near Scared Heart Academy. A
> student causally crossing the street was hit by a car going faster
> then the speed limit permits. That student is now a patent at Mu-
> nicipal Hospital, but his injuries are not to serious. He can look
> foreword to getting out of the hospital soon. Eventually he will
> recover completely excerpt for a vary small scar on his shoulder.
> Even that may disappear latter, according to his doctor.

Part Two

1. Before you let anybody else see what you have _____
   written, do you reread it, searching for misspellings?

2. As you worked with the paragraph above, did _____
   you examine it with more care than you normally use when rechecking the spellings in
   what you write?

*Compare your answers with those given in the box
on page 13.*

WHY PROOFREAD?

By striking the wrong key on her typewriter, a student wrote that she
was born, not in 1965, but in 1065. Another student wrote: "When I first
saw her, she was standing on a coroner waiting for a buss."

If such misspellings are sins, then everybody is a sinner at one time or another. That includes not only students, ranging from the worst to the very best, but also the publishers of textbooks and even of dictionaries. A college textbook—for composition classes, no less—has been caught printing *middle* as *muddle* (in big boldface type); and even a dictionary, also intended for college students, has been caught spelling *uranium* without an *r* (again in big boldface type)!

Indeed, to be human is to misspell—at least occasionally. A ringing phone leads you to strike the wrong key on a typewriter. A slamming door makes you forget to dot an *i*. Or a pleasant daydream distracts you into writing *to* for *too*. As a result, you, being human, misspell a word.

Far more serious than misspelling a word is failing to notice that you have misspelled it. Failing to find the misspelling before somebody else finds it—that is getting caught with your spelling down. Not misspelling, but getting caught—that is what is embarrassing.

In effect, there is always a race between the writer and the reader to find misspellings, a race which you, the writer, can never win if you do not even run. That is why, before you let anybody see what you have written, you should reread it carefully, searching out the misspellings which are almost certainly in it. They hide; you seek. In brief, proofread whatever you write.

WHAT PROOFREADING IS

Reading and proofreading are not the same thing. When you read, you try to get the meaning of what has been written, thus focusing your attention on the thread of thought running through the words that are before your eyes. You concentrate so much on the thought that you pay little attention to the words themselves. On the other hand, when you proofread, you concentrate more on the words than on the thought. Put in another way, when you proofread, you search not for meanings but for misspellings. You seek not ideas but words with letters improperly combined.

When you merely read, you often glance only at the outer shells of words and fail to see, inside them, the individual letters that form them. Indeed, you can get meaning from only a half shell:

LITTLE JACK HORNER

You recognize the words here even though you cannot see the individual letters well enough to identify them positively. You cannot distinguish here between L, I, and J; between O and Q; between C and G; and between R and B. Even though you cannot be sure that these words are spelled right, you can easily "read" them as "Little Jack Horner."

As your eyes move along a line in normal reading, you do not see all the words with equal clearness. You see most clearly those near the center of your field of vision, and you see least clearly those near the edge. That fact is illustrated by this schematic diagram of a field of vision:

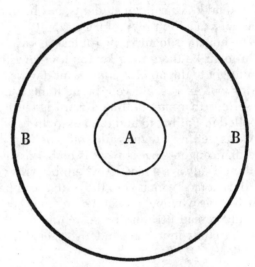

The A in the circle represents the central field of vision, where you see everything clearly; and the B represents the marginal field of vision, where you do not see things so clearly. When reading, you recognize the letters inside the words which happen to fall in the central field, but you see only the outer shells of the words which happen to fall in the marginal field. From those shells you get the meaning, as you did from the half shell of LITTLE JACK HORNER; but *you cannot verify the spellings of the words in the marginal field.*

That explains why, reading a line once, you overlook a misspelling; but reading the same line a second time, you spot the misspelling instantly. On the first reading, the misspelling happened to fall in the marginal field of your vision, where you saw only the shell of the word; but on the second reading it fell into the central field, where you saw the individual letters forming the insides of the word—its guts. Now you see why, when reading for meaning, you may utilize the full field of your vision, but, when proofreading, you should limit yourself to the center of the field. That is because you are almost certain to overlook the misspellings which happen to fall into the B area of your vision, out near the edges of the field.

If you are to rely upon the central field for proofreading, you should discover how wide that field is. The triangle of letters at the end of this paragraph will enable you to measure its width. First look at the top of the triangle. Then read down, one line at a time, until you come to a line where you cannot identify all the letters at a *single* glance, without even the tiniest movement of your eyes. The line just above the one where you cannot identify all the letters with one glance is as long as the area of your central vision is wide:

Letters	Number of Letters
o	1
qa	2
gky	3
hsxn	4
pzuvk	5
cgnokd	6
bqxapgh	7
osydzexm	8
mdikhogur	9
wjsqyxoagm	10
uzmjbphdbht	11
fwnocdnqxayn	12
tmshwigzodehm	13

ANSWERS, PRETEST 1

The misspelled words are:

Scared for *Sacred*   *foreword* for *forward*
causally for *casually*   *excerpt* for *except*
then for *than*   *vary* for *very*
patent for *patient*   *latter* for *later*
to for *too*

1. If you do not reread your work, searching for misspellings, you are not yet dealing responsibly with your problems in spelling.

2. If you examined the paragraph with more care than you normally use when rechecking your work, then the number of misspellings that you overlooked in the paragraph is probably smaller than you overlook when you recheck your own writing.

If you always recheck the spellings in your own work with as much care as you searched for misspellings in that paragraph and if, in addition, you found all the misspellings in that paragraph, then skip this chapter, and take the next pretest. Otherwise, study this chapter.

Different people have central visions of different widths, but a span about six letters wide is average. If you now believe that your own span of accurate vision is much wider than that, you should measure it again on the triangle of letters. The chances are that your first measurement was faulty because, without knowing it, you moved your eyes as you examined a line.

Anyhow, if your field of vision is about average, you should move your eyes along a line at the rate of about six letters per glance when, instead of reading, you are proofreading. If you "bite off" more than six letters per glance, you are likely to see some letters indistinctly and, as a result, to confuse such words as *premedicated* and *premeditated, coroner* and *corner, then* and *than.* You will be seeing word-shells rather than letter-shapes, and you will therefore almost certainly overlook some careless misspellings.

As a final demonstration of the difference between reading and proofreading, look at the next line:

When mispellings hide, you seek.

If, using your full field of vision, you read that line, you probably got its meaning with only two glances:

1	2
When mispellings hide,	you seek.

But if, examining each part of the line with your central vision, you proofread, you may have needed six glances:

1	2	3	4	5	6
When	mispell	ings	hide,	you	seek.

That closer examination of the line may have revealed something which you had not previously noticed: an error in the spelling of *misspellings.* (The correct form is *misspellings,* not *mispellings.*)

HOW MUCH PROOFREADING?

If, before somebody else sees what you have written, you never review it yourself, you are certain to lose the race between writer and reader in finding misspellings. You will also lose if you glance at your work only once, using the full field of your vision to get through it quickly. At least some misspellings, fiendish little gremlins that they are, will remain hidden in the outer fringes of your vision but will jump into the central vision of your reader—errors that are obvious to the reader, though they, gremlin-like, eluded you.

Of course the most thorough rechecking of what you have written requires that you go over it more than once. In at least one rereading, you should look ONLY for misspellings, and this rereading should be done so slowly that you bring every letter within the narrow range of your central vision. In other rereadings, which may be at a much faster pace, you may be alert to other things besides spellings—such things as punctuation, sentence structure, and style.

Repeated rechecking of written work is customary for professional writers and editors. Only amateurs expect their work to be error-free. Editors of one outstanding magazine recheck their copy, not once or twice, but ten times before the plates for printing are finally made—and still mistakes occasionally slip through. Naïve indeed are the students and other amateurs who dash off a piece of writing and turn it in without checking it even once.

To develop your skill as a searcher for misspellings, do the next exercise

EXERCISE 1

Underline the misspellings in these sentences:

1. This diary owns some prize cows.
2. He prepared his lessons throughly.
3. In an emergency, don't loose your head.
4. Where you there when it happened?
5. This elevator stops at the forth floor.
6. He bought a cartoon of cigarettes.
7. Thank you very mulch.
8. Because that had no children, they adapted one.
9. The cowboy was wearing a ten-galleon hat.
10. We ordered some new stationary from the printer.
11. For breakfast we had ham an eggs.
12. I don't know weather we should go.
13. Then the calvary charge began.
14. The trial in the woods disappeared into the underbrush.
15. She suffers from allusions of grandeur.
16. We were forced to altar our plans.
17. Precede with your conversation.
18. Advice is easy to give, but hard to take.

19. Who's home is this?
20. The men were lost in the dessert for two days.

The misspellings are listed in the box on page 19.

POSTTEST 1

Underline the misspellings in the sentences below. To make sure that you examine each word with your central vision, put a dot under each word as you verify its spelling.

1. For us to solve this problem, we must all corporate.
2. We watched cowboys ride bucking broncos while we sat on the coral fence.
3. Llewellyn told all his friends just as soon as his brook was published.
4. Laundry was swinging back and fourth on the line in the yard.
5. The trouble with him is that he cannot tell the difference between what is his and what is mime.
6. Her family was much better known then his.
7. When he was in the Army, he was a squab leader.
8. Most of all, she wanted to relax for a few days in Hawaii.
9. I remember when Elmer was just a squall child.
10. At the front of almost every book is a preface or forward to introduce the reader to the book.
11. Neither of us can do it alone, but togeather we should be able to accomplish it.
12. The cat picked up the kitten by the nap of the neck.
13. My girl is just to cute for words.
14. He merely stood their with his hands in his pockets.
15. She wore her best patient leather shoes to the party.
16. Meteorologists are sometimes known as whether men.
17. The little flaxen-haired girl had a large red ribbon in her hair.
18. What he most likes for breakfast is a high stack of girdle cakes.
19. Englishmen often prefer a cup of tee to a cup of coffee.
20. A good cartographer, curiously enough, may know nothing about carts.

The misspellings are listed in the box on page 21.

2
DEVELOPING A
SENSE OF DOUBT

PRETEST 2

Part One

Complete the spelling of the words with a blank in them. If you are not sure whether your spelling is correct, put a mark in the "D" (for "doubtful") space by the word.

D

1. Sep ___ rate the sheep from the goats. ___

2. What did you rec ___ ve for Christmas? ___

3. Has the exist ___ nce of life on Mars been proved? ___

4. To curse in church is sacr ___ l ___ gious. ___

5. He is a pro ___ essor of chemistry. ___

6. She made a def ___ n ___ te promise. ___

7. What was the occa ___ ion for the celebration? ___

8. To serve you is a priv ___ le ___ e. ___

9. What occu ___ ed next startled us. ___

10. That proc ___ dure is complicated. ___

Part Two

1. Is a dictionary within easy reach where you most often write? ___

2. When you write or revise, do you often consult your dictionary to make sure that a spelling is right? ___

Compare your answers with those given in the box
on page 23.

17

WHAT IS A SENSE OF DOUBT?

The pretest is intended to help you to measure your sense of doubt about spelling. What is a sense of doubt? It is an attitude of caution toward spelling, a tendency to be unsure about the spelling, not only of strange new words like *syringomyelia,* but also of common yet tricky words like *accommodate* and *accumulate.* With a sense of doubt, you do not overestimate your ability to spell—you realize when you get beyond your depth and therefore need the help that a dictionary can provide. A dictionary is a life preserver in a sea of spellings, a sea that is big and often tumultuous.

On the pretest you were asked to spell ten words that are very frequently misspelled, and you were asked to indicate which of your spellings you were doubtful about. If, wonder of wonders, you got all ten spellings right and also marked none of them as doubtful, then the pretest failed to measure your personal sense of doubt. If you got all spellings right but marked some as doubtful, then your sense of doubt is excessive: you worry about spellings more often than you really need to—a marvelous excess to have! If you marked as doubtful the same number of words that you misspelled, then your sense of doubt is just the right size, neither too large nor too small. Also, if you marked as doubtful precisely the words that you actually misspelled, then your sense of doubt is not only the right size, but is also accurate and therefore reliable—something you can count on to lead you to your dictionary whenever you need it. Finally, if you marked as doubtful fewer words than you actually misspelled, then your sense of doubt is too small, and it needs to be enlarged if it is to serve as a valuable instrument for improving your spelling.

HOW DOUBT CAN IMPROVE SPELLING

How a sense of doubt may affect spelling is shown by the performance of three students on a test containing a hundred and eight hard-to-spell words. The first student, who may be called Joe, was a poor speller and also had a sense of doubt that was far too small: he missed ninety-two words and marked only nine of his misspelled words as doubtful. Thus, even with the aid of a dictionary, he would have missed eighty-three words!

The second student, Jim, was also a poor speller, but he had a phenomenally good sense of doubt. Though he misspelled sixty-eight words, he marked sixty of them as doubtful. With the aid of a dictionary, he would have missed only eight words—only about a tenth as many as Joe did!

The third student, Judy, was a good speller, but she had a poor sense of doubt. She missed only ten words, and she marked only one of them as doubtful. Even with the aid of a dictionary, she would have missed nine words—one more than would have been missed by Jim, the poor speller with the good sense of doubt.*

So you see, a poor speller with a good sense of doubt is capable of making a better showing than a good speller with a poor sense of doubt. Even the best spellers often need a sense of doubt, not only when they come to unusual new words such as *chryselephantine*, but also when they come to common but tricky words such as *accumulate* (two *c*'s but one *m*), *conferred* (two *r*'s), and *deceived* (the *e* before the *i*).

A sense of doubt can be helpful in two important ways. In the first place, it can enable you to avoid misspellings, large numbers of them, just as it could have enabled Jim to avoid sixty misspellings if he had been permitted to use a dictionary while taking the test. In the second place, it can aid you in learning how to spell the very words that you are most likely to misspell.

When doubt leads you to your dictionary and you copy down the spelling found there, you have taken the first step toward learning how to spell the word. If, when you first look up a word, you study its spell-

---

*For additional statistics on the sense of doubt in students who took this test, see pages 158-159.

ANSWERS, EXERCISE 1

The words misspelled in the exercise are correctly spelled here:

1. dairy	8. adopted	14. trail
2. thoroughly	9. ten-gallon	15. illusions
3. lose	10. stationery	16. alter
4. Were	11. and	17. Proceed
5. fourth	12. whether	18. _____
6. carton	13. cavalry	19. Whose
7. much		20. desert

Go on to the next chapter if you overlooked no misspellings in this exercise. If you did overlook any, review this chapter and take the posttest before going on.

ing, trying to fix that spelling in your mind forever, you may never need to look up that particular word again—you will have learned to spell it! Even if you do not learn its spelling the first time, your sense of doubt can lead you back to the dictionary again and again, repeatedly, until you *do* learn to spell it. When you discover that the dictionary spelling is just what you thought, in advance, that it was, then you can assume that you have learned to spell the word, and you may never have to look it up again. Your sense of doubt will have done its job for that word, and you may thereafter be sure of your spelling of that word. Thus a sense of doubt is a self-liquidating instrument for improving spelling: it automatically disappears when it is no longer needed.

INCREASING YOUR SENSE OF DOUBT

This book has been designed to help you to increase your sense of doubt and its reliability.

You began the process when you took the pretest for this chapter, which, by enabling you to measure your sense of doubt, revealed whether or not you need to increase it. Almost all students who used earlier editions of this book did need to increase their sense of doubt, and many needed to increase it enormously. You should seek to increase it if you did not mark as doubtful all the words that you misspelled, and you should increase it greatly if you did not mark as doubtful most of the words that you missed.

In another way, too, that pretest may have helped: its hard-to-spell words may have proved that you are overconfident about your ability to spell. Of course a sense of doubt cannot be increased until its principal enemy, overconfidence, is first recognized and then decreased. Perhaps the difficult words convinced you that you cannot rely so much upon your intuitions about spelling—that you should consult your dictionary far more often in the future than you have in the past.

The chapter that you are now reading further emphasizes the fact that an increased sense of doubt may quickly lead to a decreased number of misspellings—and eventually to learning the spelling of the very words which you now miss.

Later chapters, too, have been planned to aid you in increasing your sense of doubt. Most later chapters discuss the really important trouble spots in spelling—the precise spots that you should be doubtful about when you encounter them in your writing. So, as you work through these later chapters, you will begin to recognize automatically the spellings that you should be suspicious about. Then these spellings, when recognized as troublesome, will serve as warnings to you: they will be like flashing red lights, signaling that you should stop and consult your dictionary before going on.

Finally, in the pretests, exercises, and posttests for the later chapters you will find a "D" space by every word—a space for you to mark if you are doubtful about the spelling of the word. This space leads you, time afer time, to decide whether or not you are doubtful about your spellings. By thus repeatedly making decisions about the certainty or doubtfulness of your spellings, you will develop the *habit* of being suspicious about the troublesome spots in your spellings.

A healthy sense of doubt is a wonderful thing to have. It can—more quickly than anything else—enable you to avoid misspellings. On top of that, it can gradually lead you to learn the correct spellings of the particular words that you personally have the most trouble with. Indeed, if there is a magic formula for the improvement of spelling, it is this:

Doubt + Dictionary = Good Spelling

The sense of doubt alone is useless unless it leads one to the dictionary, and the presence of the dictionary is useless without the sense of doubt to stimulate its use. Both are needed, just as both legs are needed for walking. When a good sense of doubt is used with a readily accessible dictionary, they come close to producing miracles in spelling.

* * *

ANSWERS, POSTTEST 1

The words misspelled in the posttest are correctly spelled here:

1. cooperate	8. _____	14. there
2. corral	9. small	15. patent
3. book	10. foreword	16. weather
4. forth	11. together	17. _____
5. mine	12. nape	18. griddle
6. than	13. too	19. tea
7. squad		20. _____

Do the next exercise, and then take the following posttest.

EXERCISE 2

1. Other things being equal, can poor spellers with a good sense of doubt write with as few misspellings as good spellers with a poor sense of doubt? ____

2. If there is a magic formula for a quick improvement in spelling, what is it? _____

   _____

3. Should you be doubtful about the spelling (a) of strange new words like *proceleusmatic*, (b) of common but troublesome words like *accumulate*, or (c) of both? ____

4. Can a good sense of doubt be developed more quickly than the spelling of all the common English words can be learned? ____

5. How does an increased familiarity with the chief trouble spots in English spelling help to increase and make more reliable a sense of doubt? _____

   _____

6. Why do most of the later exercises have "D" spaces? _____

   _____

7. Most habits are developed if an action is repeated again and again. Can the habit of consulting a dictionary as an aid to spelling be developed in any other way? _____ ____

For suggested answers see box on page 25.

POSTTEST 2

Complete the spelling of the words with a blank in them, and mark the "D" space if you are doubtful about the spelling which you choose.

D

1. Do you bel __ ve in Santa Claus?   ____
2. Is it caused by heredity or envi __ ment?   ____
3. "In the begi __ ing was the Word."   ____
4. He ach __ ved his goal.   ____
5. That is a fa __ inating book.   ____
6. How inte __ igent she is!   ____
7. Come home i __ ediately.   ____
8. The dogs p __ sued the fox.   ____
9. She teaches gram __ r in school.   ____
10. His intoxication was notic __ ble.   ____

For answers see box on page 27.

ANSWERS, PRETEST 2

One

1. separate	6. definite
2. receive	7. occasion
3. existence	8. privilege
4. sacrilegious	9. occurred
5. professor	10. procedure

Two

1. If a dictionary is not within easy reach where you most often write, you are not physically equipped to do a good job of spelling, for consulting a dictionary for spellings that you are not sure of is an essential part of being a good speller.

2. Having a dictionary handy will do no good unless you consult it often, especially to make sure that a spellling is right.

If all your answers on this test are correct, go on now to the next chapter. If not, study this chapter first.

3

SPELLING PROBLEMS: PERSONAL AND VERBAL

PRETEST 3

1. Is English the language that you learned first? ___

2. Is your vision up to par, at least with the aid of corrective lenses? ___

3. Have your eyes been examined professionally within the last two years? ___

4. Is a dictionary within easy reach at the place where you most often write? ___

5. Do you frequently consult your dictionary for a spelling when you write or revise? ___

6. Before you let anybody else see what you have written, do you search for misspellings in it? ___

7. Do you regard correct spelling as so important that you are willing to devote considerable time to its achievement? ___

8. Do your peers—the people that you spend most of your free time with—regard spelling as important enough to justify the spending of considerable time in studying it? ___

For answers see box on page 29.

PERSONAL AND VERBAL PROBLEMS IN SPELLING

The problems in spelling are of two basic kinds: personal and verbal. Personal problems are to be found in the person trying to spell, not in the word that he or she is trying to spell, while verbal problems are to be found in the word itself—say, in its peculiar combination of letters.

Typical of the personal problems are such things as you were questioned about in the pretest: the influence of a native language other than English, the unknown handicap of poor vision, and a "don't-care" attitude which keeps you from proofreading your work and also from consulting a dictionary as often as you should. Such personal problems are extremely important because, until you solve them, you probably cannot solve the other kind of problems, the verbal ones.

The verbal problems are chiefly the result of the inconsistent ways that letters are combined to form words. For instance, why is *pneumonia* spelled with a *p*? Why isn't *through* spelled *thru*? And why is the same pronunciation often given two different spellings, as in *principal* and *principle*? Such illogical combinations of letters are unquestionably problems, verbal problems which can be solved *if* the personal problems are solved first.

SOLVING THE PERSONAL PROBLEMS

(1.) If English is not the first language that you learned, your spelling of the words in that other language may interfere with your spelling in English. This problem may be big, if you have been working with English for just a year or two, or small, if you have been at it for several years. In either case, you should consult with a teacher of English as a foreign language—preferably somebody who is a native speaker of English and who, in addition, has had professional training in phonetics, the science dealing with the sounds of language. Such a person, who can be found on most college campuses, can help you more than anybody else with this problem, regardless of whether it is big or small. Ask your

---

ANSWERS, EXERCISE 2

1. Yes.
2. Doubt + dictionary = good spelling.
3. c.
4. Yes.
5. By making one doubtful about the words with trouble spots.†
6. To develop your sense of doubt.†
7. No.

---

†This is not the only acceptable answer.

teacher to recommend such a consultant or (if qualified) to serve as such a consultant.

(2, 3.) A person with less than perfect vision is almost certain to be a less than perfect speller. That is because spelling is a visual art: a spelling is something to be seen, not heard or sensed in any other way. A correct spelling "looks" right, and an incorrect one "looks" wrong. That is why proofreading can be no better than the visual sharpness of the proofreader. So you, if you want to spell well, must be sure that your vision is perfect or as nearly perfect as an oculist, ophthalmologist, or optometrist can make it. If you have not had a professional examination of your eyes within the last two years, you should have one as soon as possible. Can you *today* make an appointment for it?

(4, 5.) If a dictionary is not within easy reach where you most often write, you will not consult it for spellings often enough. Getting out of your chair, walking part of the way across the room, or walking into some other room—having to do these things will inhibit your use of the dictionary and thus increase the number of misspellings. Therefore it is a good idea for you, today or at least by tonight, to put a dictionary within easy reach where you most often write. (You may also want to consider the purchase of a smaller and therefore more portable book for carrying to the places where you less often write: a pocket thesaurus, word-finder, or spelling dictionary.) And you should also resolve—why not also today?—to check your spellings in such books much more often in the future than you have in the past.

(6.) If you still are not searching for misspellings in what you write, you still have a personal problem that you are ignoring—a problem sure to cause you embarrassment and perhaps to cost you a job in the future. The habit of proofreading can be developed only by doing—only by actually proofreading whatever you write for others to read.

(7, 8.) If you (partly because of your peers) do not regard good spelling as important enough to spend some time on it, then your spelling cannot improve. If it is poor now, it will remain poor for as long as your "don't-care" attitude lasts. That poor spelling can, of course, hurt you. It can keep you from getting top grades in school and from gaining professional advancement in all the years after you graduate (if, indeed, you *do* graduate). It can damage you socially, lowering your personal prestige. Indeed, it can hold you back, frustrating you, in almost every phase of your life—and do it for your entire life.

A SUMMARY OF THE PROBLEMS

PERSONAL PROBLEMS

1. CARELESSNESS may be a problem if you do not reread your work so carefully that every letter is brought within the small area of greatest accuracy at the center of your field of vision.

2. OVERCONFIDENCE may be a problem if you do not often consult a dictionary kept at the place where you most often write.

3. POOR VISION may be a problem if you have not had a professional examination of your eyes within the last two years.

4. A FOREIGN BACKGROUND may be a problem if English is not the language that you learned first.

VERBAL PROBLEMS

1. UNSTRESSED VOWELS are illustrated by the capitalized *a* in *sepArate, e* in *catEgory, i* in *origInal, o* in *sophOmore,* and *u* in *guttUral.*

2. OMITTED LETTERS are illustrated by the capitalized *c* in *aCquit, d* in *canDidate, n* in *columN,* and *t* in *ofTen.*

3. ADDED LETTERS are illustrated by the capitalized *d* in *drownDed, e* in *disastErous, l* in *untilL,* and *p* in *opPinion.* (All those capitalized letters are wrong.)

ANSWERS, POSTTEST 2

1. believe	6. intelligent
2. environment	7. immediately
3. beginning	8. pursued
4. achieved	9. grammar
5. fascinating	10. noticeable

Compare your answers in this posttest with those in the earlier pretest, noticing whether or not your sense of doubt has increased.

4. IDENTICAL PRONUNCIATIONS are illustrated by such pairs as *capital* and *capitol, complement* and *compliment, principal* and *principle, their* and *there,* and *to* and *too.*

5. SIMILAR PRONUNCIATIONS are illustrated by such pairs as *affect* and *effect, formally* and *formerly, precede* and *proceed,* and *statue* and *statute.*

6. IE or EI? That problem is illustrated by such words as *believe* and *deceive, field* and *freight,* and *siege* and *seize.*

7. FINAL DOUBLING is illustrated by the contrast between *equipped* and *equipment, hopping* and *hoping, preferred* and *preference,* and *shipped* and *worshiped.*

8. FINAL E is illustrated by the contrasts between *amusement* and *amusing, changeable* and *changing, ninety* and *ninth,* and *terrible* and *terribly.*

9. ASSIMILATIVE DOUBLING is illustrated by such words as *accumulate, affix, aggregate, allure, annex, appoint, assign,* and *attract.*

10. ADDITIVE DOUBLING is illustrated by *drunkenness, misstatement, really, suddenness,* and *unnaturally.*

11. FINAL Y is illustrated by the contrasts between *alleys* and *allies, burying* and *burial, magnifying* and *magnified,* and *Sallys* and *sallies.*

12. OTHER FINAL LETTERS are illustrated by the contrasts between *elf* and *elves, panics* and *panicked, pianos* and *potatoes,* and *thief* and *thieves.*

13. INTERNAL DOUBLING is illustrated by *brilliant, bulletin, curriculum, embarrass, fallacy, parallel, territory, tobacco,* and *vacuum.*

14. COMPETING SPELLINGS are illustrated by *abridgment* and *abridgement, draftsman* and *draughtsman, fiber* and *fibre, humor* and *humour, judgment* and *judgement,* and *through* and *thru.*

15.   COMPOUND WORDS are illustrated by the contrast between *camp chair* and *campfire, coon dog* and *coonskin, dive bomber* and *dive-bomb, feather bed* and *featherbedding,* and *fish warden* and *fishwife.*

NOTE: Each of these verbal problems is discussed in a following chapter.

ANSWERS, PRETEST 3

If you answered all those questions "yes," skip this chapter and go on to the next one. If you answered any "no," read the first part of this chapter and also the numbered portions dealing with your "no" answers.

4

PERSONALIZED
LIST OF
MISSPELLINGS

At the end of this book are spaces to be filled in with words that you actually misspell. That is why the list is "personalized"—no other list will be just like yours.

Begin the list by putting into it—spelled correctly—all words now marked as incorrect in the pretests, exercises, and posttests in earlier chapters of this book. Also include all words marked as misspelled in papers recently returned to you by your teachers. And, as you continue working with this book, continue to list the misspellings found in your pretests, exercises, posttests, and other papers.

In all probability, merely listing these words will not be enough to enable you to learn to spell them—the thing that you really want to do. If the list remains short (say, only one or two dozen words long), then you may memorize the spellings. Do that by writing each word again and again until you get the *habit* of spelling it correctly. Or when you discover what part of the word you tend to misspell, you may emphasize the correct spelling of that part by capitalizing it when you copy the word. Or you may make the troublesome letter(s) several times as large as the other letters in the word, thus:

SEP **A** RATE

If you copy a word like that on a small scrap of paper and place the paper along the edge of your mirror, you will see it, with its trouble spot enlarged, every time you powder your nose or shave. Keep that word there until you are sure that you know how to spell it, trouble spot and all. Then put a new word there for painless memorizing. If your personalized list of misspellings remains fairly short, you may continue this process until you have mastered all the words on it.

Or, instead of memorizing, you may perfer to use mnemonic devices as an aid for mastering the listed words. A mnemonic (pronounced *ni-MON-ic*) device is a reminder—something to help you remember. It is like a calendar filled with appointments or like a string tied around your finger. Most precisely, it is a set of mental associations to help you to spell a word. These associations become so closely tied to the word that, whenever you think of the word, you also think of the associations, and the associations remind you how to spell the word.

For instance, suppose that you are trying to distinguish between the two words *desert* and *dessert*. One of them has a single *s;* the other has two *s's.* The one which refers to an arid region, such as the Sahara, has only one *s* (and so does *Sahara* itself), while the one which refers to the last course of a meal, such as strawberry shortcake, has two *s's* (and so does *strawberry shortcake* itself).

Or suppose that you are trying to force yourself to remember that the word *vaccine* and two *c's* in it. You should have no trouble if you recall that most *vaccines* are measured in cubic centimeters or cc's.

If your list of misspellings becomes so long that you do not want to work with only one word at a time—as you must when memorizing or using mnemonic devices—then you may (with the help of the alphabetized "List of Frequent Misspellings," beginning on page 176) classify your misspellings, and then work on them a class or a group at a time—one kind of trouble spot at a time. Not every word in your personalized list may be in that later list, but enough will almost certainly be there to show you which trouble spots are causing most of your mistakes.

Next to each word in that later list (Appendix F) is the number of a chapter in this book dealing with the trouble spot(s) in the word. Put that number next to the same word in your personalized list, and you will, in effect, be classifying that word. When you have thus numbered all possible words in your personalized list, you may discover that only a few verbal problems are causing numerous misspellings—for instance, that only three chapter numbers are next to twenty-nine misspellings. Of course the thing to do then is to work with those three chapters, which explain the underlying verbal problems, rather than with those twenty-nine misspellings. Some chapters provide a rule which applies to hundreds or even thousands of individual spellings—a real shortcut for mastering many words quickly.

Now you see how to compile your own personalized list of misspellings and, after it is compiled, how to use it. Before going on to the next chapter, start it, listing your words in Appendix G at the back of this book. Then, as you work with later chapters and as teachers mark other misspellings in your later papers, add those later misspellings to the list, keeping it up to date.

PART II PRONUNCIATION AS A GUIDE

As we spell a word, we are often guided by how it is pronounced. When writing, we often say in our minds the words which we are putting down on paper, and the sounds which we thus "hear" serve as guides for the letters that we put on the paper in front of us.

Sometimes pronunciation is thus an excellent guide for spelling, leading us quickly and easily to the spellings which are correct. That is true of words like **bad, bed,** and **bit,** which are spelled precisely as they are pronounced. But at other times pronunciation is not a reliable guide. Then, instead of leading us toward a correct spelling, it misleads us toward a misspelling. That is true of words like **laugh, mnemonics,** and **philosophy,** where spelling and pronunication are quite different from each other. Learning when to rely upon pronunciation as a guide—**and when not to rely upon it**—can therefore be a major step forward in the improvement of spelling.

The next six chapters deal with six situations in which pronunciation is **not** a reliable guide to spelling. In these situations, which you can easily learn one at a time, pronunciation is more likely to mislead you to an incorrect spelling than it is to lead you to a correct one. That is why its guidance is to be accepted cautiously, if at all, in dealing with these six trouble spots in spelling.

Why is pronunciation an unreliable guide for dealing with these trouble spots? It is unreliable because there is not a one-to-one relationship between sounds and letters in English. One sound in pronunciation is not always represented by one letter in spelling. And the opposite is true: one letter in spelling does not always represent one sound in pronunciation.

Indeed, there has never been such a one-to-one relationship between sound and letter in English. When, many centuries ago, the language was first written, it was written in a borrowed alphabet which had fewer letters than the language had sounds. So the match between sound and letter has never been perfect. Furthermore, unless English adopts a new and expanded alphabet—a most unlikely occurrence!—the match never will be perfect.

Several peculiarities of English spelling are a result of attempts to represent our spoken language with an alphabet having too few letters. One way in which early scribes attempted to solve that problem can be illustrated by comparing the sounds and letters coming first in **tea, he,** and **the.** Those words obviously begin with three different sounds, but are spelled with only two different letters, **t** and **h.** The third sound (in **the**), for which our alphabet still provides no letter, is spelled by a combination of letters, **t** and **h,** which else-where (as in **tea** and **he**) represent other sounds. By thus using combinations of letters, rather than single letters, to represent some of its sounds, English spelling has overcome the shortage of letters in its alphabet. As a result, how-ever, there is not always a one-to-one relationship between sound and letter. That is a basic reason why pronunciation is not always a reliable guide to spelling.

Another basic reason is that English spelling began to become standard-ized or fixed centuries ago, while English pronunciation has continued to change. Because spelling has stood still while pronunciation has moved on, the differences between spelling and pronunciation have grown greater and greater with every passing century. At one time, long ago, the spellings of **laugh** and **knife** were fairly accurate representations of their pronunciations. For ex-ample, both the **k** and the **e** in **knife** were pronounced. Since then those two sounds in the word have become silent, but the two letters representing them in the spelling have persisted like fossils. In the same way other sounds are now in the process of becoming silent, but the letters representing them will no doubt persist, like fossils, in the spelling of the future. An illustration of a disappearing sound whose letter is likely to survive is the **d** of **and,** especially in such expressions as "ham 'n' eggs."

Because our alphabet does not have enough letters to represent all the sounds in our language and because our spellings have not changed whenever our pronunciations have changed, at least six trouble spots in spelling have developed—trouble spots which are now to be considered one by one.

5

UNSTRESSED VOWELS

PRETEST 5

Put the needed vowel in the blank. Mark the "D" column if you are doubtful about that vowel.

		D
1.	Two synon___mous words	___
2.	Sold at great sacr___fice	___
3.	The calend___r on the wall	___
4.	The long-antic___pated day	___
5.	Worked with dilig___nce	___
6.	A good mag___zine to read	___
7.	The oldest grave in the cemet___ry	___
8.	Overcame all obst___cles	___
9.	His vulg___r remark	___
10.	The Declaration of Independ___nce	___

For answers see box on page 37.

UNSTRESSED VOWELS AS TROUBLEMAKERS

No sounds in English cause more trouble in spelling than unstressed vowels do. They are the fiends in the language, tripping up writers more often than any other sounds do. An analysis of more than 31,000 misspellings by college students reveals that over 4,000 of those misspellings were caused by unstressed vowels—at least one misspelling out of every eight. In that same sampling of misspellings by college students, 196 words were misspelled at least thirty times each, and sixty-one of

35

those words, almost a third of them, were misspelled because of their unstressed vowels. Clearly, then, no verbal problem in spelling is greater than the problem of unstressed vowels, and therefore no problem deserves more attention than this one does. These vowels are, let it be repeated for emphasis, the fiends of the language.

HOW TO SPOT THE FIENDS

What is an unstressed vowel? It is a vowel pronounced like the *a* of *sofa*. It is a faint, blurred "uh." It is spoken softly, with only a tiny bit of loudness—much less than that used in pronouncing the *o* of *sofa*, which is a stressed vowel. Though it resembles the stressed "uh" sound in such words as *hut, rush, tub, blood,* and *ton,* it is uttered more quietly, with less force. It is, in effect, a "hushed" sound, little more than a whisper.

In normal speech we obviously do not pronounce all vowels with the same loudness. For instance, we say the first more loudly than the second in *drama, monster, garden,* and *Reba.* In contrast, we say the second more loudly than the first in *alone, before,* and *suggest.* Actually say those seven words aloud, and you will begin to recognize the unstressed vowels in them: the weak, indistinct "uh."

Another way to become aware of the unstressed "uh" is to say aloud these two sentences:

> The first letter of the alphabet is *a.*

> What a game that was!

In the first of those sentences *a* was stressed and therefore pronounced clearly; in the second, it was unstressed and therefore mumbled—a faint, blurred "uh," as in *sofa.*

For additional practice in spotting unstressed vowels (and also as a test of your skill in spotting them), do the next exercise.

EXERCISE 5A

Put a dot under the unstressed vowels in these words:

account	sustain	Ezra
upon	confess	gratitude
oppose	unwind	nasal
elusive	kangaroo	magazine
obtrude	tidal	televise
appear	policy	salmon

For answers see box on page 39.

Though that "uh" is by far the most troublesome of the unstressed vowel sounds, it is not the only one causing grief in spelling. The other one is an unstressed *i* sound, as in *solId*. That sound is troublesome because it is spelled in several different ways: with *a* in *privAte*, *equippAge*, *terrAce*, and *palAce*; with *e* in *privEt*, *privilEge*, and *knowlEdge*; with *i* in *porrIdge*, *placId*, and *morbId*; and with *y* in *prettY*, *piracY*, *loudlY*, and *urgencY*. As those examples demonstrate, there is not a one-to-one relationship between the pronunciation of that sound and the spelling of that sound. That sound is spelled in various ways, inconsistently and therefore unpredictably.

WHY THE FIENDS ARE FIENDS

The unstressed vowel sounds, both *i* and "uh," are major troublemakers because they are spelled in English with so many different letters. Already you have seen that the sound of unstressed *i* may be represented by at least four different letters:

The sound	Its spelling	In the word
	a	privAte
i	e	privEt
	i	solId
	y	piracY

And, as the next diagram shows, the sound of unstressed "uh" may be represented in an even wider variety of confusing ways:

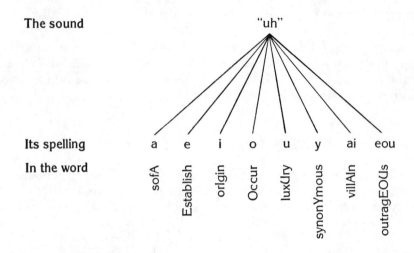

The sound	"uh"
Its spelling	a e i o u y ai eou
In the word	sofA Establish orIgin Occur luxUry synonYmous villAIn outragEOUs

In more detail, unstressed "uh" is spelled with *a* in *sofA, sodA, Above, Amount, sepArate,* and *ecstAsy;* with *e* in *Establish, elEmEnt,* and *existEnce;* with *i* in *fatalIty, notIfy,* and *orIgin;* with *o* in *Occur, oppOsite,* and *winsOme;* with *u* in *Unseen, guttUral,* and *luxUry.* In addition, it is spelled with pairs of letters in *famOUs* and *villAIn;* and even by combinations of three letters, as in *outragEOUs.* No wonder the spelling of this sound is tricky! Indeed, its spelling is utterly outrageous!

HOW THE FIENDS BECAME FIENDS

Unstressed vowels became a problem for a reason already described on page 36: their spellings became fixed centuries ago, but their pronunciations have continued to change during the intervening centuries. In more detail, many vowels which are now unstressed were earlier stressed and were therefore pronounced loud and clear.

That was true of the *a* of *sofa,* which was pronounced a loud and clear "ah," the same "ah" that a doctor asks you to say when he wants to examine your wide-open mouth. But that great big "ah" in *sofa* has now, through a loss of stress, been reduced to a little "uh," mumbled faintly. Indeed, all vowel sounds, when they have lost stress, have become a mumbled "uh" or, less frequently, a mumbled *i.* That is why these unstressed vowels are spelled in so many different ways—because they were once pronounced, loudly and clearly, in all those different ways.

What happened may also be illustrated by comparing the pronunciations and spellings of *victorious, victory,* and *victery.* In *victorious* the first *o* is stressed and therefore is clearly heard as an *o* or "oh." In *victory* the *o* is not stressed and therefore is heard only as a mumbled "uh." Notice that *o* remains in the spelling of *victory,* though it has disappeared from the pronunication of the word. In *victery,* finally, the *o* has disappeared from the spelling too, as it logically might. But *victery* is of course, a misspelling—the very kind of misspelling that unstressed vowels fiendishly provoke.

HOW TO FIGHT THE FIENDS

There are three chief ways for solving the problem of spelling the unstressed vowels. The first, which should be tried first, is to use mnemonic devices,* especially a single device that can solve the problem for many words with unstressed vowels. The second, which should be tried next, is to memorize the spelling of the comparatively few words with unstressed vowels that you actually have trouble with—a memorizing which can be aided by graphic devices, such as capitalized letters. The third way to solve the problem, to be used as a last resort for the

---

*Mnemonic devices are explained on page 30.

ANSWERS, EXERCISE 5A

account	sustain	Ezra
upon	confess	gratitude
oppose	unwind	nasal
elusive	kangaroo	magazine
obtrude	tidal	televise
appear	policy	salmon

remaining words that are troublesome, is to increase your sense of doubt about these very tricky spellings.

1. MNEMONIC DEVICES

A single simple mnemonic device can guide you in the spelling of numerous words pronounced with an unstressed vowel—all words which, like *victory* and *victorious,* have two forms with different pronunciations. In one form a vowel, like the *o* of *victory,* is unstressed, but in the other form the same vowel is stressed, as in *victorious,* where it is clearly pronounced as an *o* instead of an "uh." The *victorious* form can therefore guide you in spelling the *victory* form right: with an *o* before the *r.*

In the same way, the two forms of the following words will enable you to get their spellings right:

authOr–authOrity	labOratory–labOrious
defInite–defIne	luxUry–luxUrious
democrAcy–democrAt	medIcine–medIcinal
fallAcy–fallAcious	memOry–memOrial
fantAsy–fantAstic	navigAble–navigAte
frivOlous–frivOlity	orIgin–orIginal
grammAr–grammAtical	relAtive–relAtion
histOry–histOrical	symbOl–symbOlic
hypocrIsy–hypocrIte	tolerAnt–tolerAte
ignOrant–ignOre	victOry–victOrious.

Saying those pairs aloud will show you how pronouncing the second form can guide you in spelling the first form. For example, the unstressed vowel in *authOr* must be spelled with an *o* because the corresponding vowel in *authOrity* is clearly pronounced with an *o.* Likewise the unstressed vowel in *defInite* must be spelled with an *i* because the corresponding vowel in *defIne* is clearly pronounced with an *i.* And so on through all twenty of those pairs. (There are many more than these twenty pairs in the language, but these are enough to show how this mnemonic device works.)

So far each pair has been used as an aid for spelling only one unstressed vowel, but some pairs can be used as an aid for the spelling of more than one unstressed vowel. *Democracy–democrat* is an example of a pair with such double usefulness. Just as *democrAcy–democrAt* shows *a* as the correct spelling for one unstressed vowel, so does *demOcrat–demOcracy* show that *o* is the correct spelling for a second unstressed vowel in the pair. In the same way, just as *hypocrIsy–hypocrIte* shows *i* as the spelling for one unstressed vowel, so does *hypOcrite–hypOcrisy* shows that *o* is the spelling for a second unstressed vowel in the pair. And the same is true for some (but not all) other pairs.

For practice in using this mnemonic device as an aid for spelling unstressed vowels, do the next exercise.

EXERCISE 5B

In the blanks to the left, put the proper vowel. In the blanks to the right, put a form of the same word where that vowel is stressed. Example:

or _a_ torical   orAte _____

1. arist __ crat   _____
2. cour __ ge   _____
3. econ __ my   _____
4. hist __ ry   _____
5. med __ cine   _____
6. mel __ dy   _____
7. ment __ l   _____
8. pres __ dent   _____
9. profess __ r   _____
10. prov __ cation   _____
11. res __ lute   _____
12. rot __ ry   _____
13. tel __ graph   _____
14. temp __ st   _____
15. torr __ nt   _____
16. vulg __ r   _____

For answers see box on page 43.

All words with unstressed vowels causing trouble in spelling do not, unfortunately, have two forms that can be used as a guide for spelling. Indeed, some of the words most frequently misspelled because of their unstressed vowel do not have two such forms. That is why other mnemonic devices must be designed for them, a different device for every different word. Below are examples of some devices which have been dreamed up for some of the most fiendish of these words:

	Device
attendance	Would you like to ATTEND a DANCE?
business	SIN is in buSINess.
disease	To be DISeased is to be UNcomfortable.
existence	Prefer an easy existence, one with three *e*'s in it: ExistEncE. Or put TEN in exisTENce.
fundamental	Associate *fundamental* with *foundation* or *foundational,* for they have closely related meanings. Then notice that the troublesome vowel in *fundamental* is clearly pronounced as *a* in *foundAtion(al)*. So it should be spelled *a* in *fundamental,* too. This alignment of the two words may also be helpful:

foundAtional
fundAmental.

Those are samples of mnemonic devices that you may be able to dream up for the fiendish words in your personalized list of misspellings (page 181). Right now, while these devices are still fresh in your mind, look at those words in your list, let your imagination run wild, and try to come up with some mental associations that will help you get those words correct in the future. The next exercise provides spaces for your own words and your own mnemonic devices for them. Fill in the spaces now, before reading on.

EXERCISE 5C

Words   **Mnemonic Devices**

_____   _____

                       _____

                       _____

_____   _____

                       _____

                       _____

Words   Mnemonic Devices

_____   _____

                                         _____

                                         _____

_____   _____

                                         _____

                                         _____

                                         _____

_____   _____

                                         _____

                                         _____

_____   _____

                                         _____

                                         _____

ANSWERS, EXERCISE 5B

1. aristOcracy
2. courAgeous
3. econOmical
4. histOrical,
   histOrian
5. medIcinal
6. melOdic
7. mentAlity
8. presIde

9. professOrial
10. provOke
11. resOlve
12. rotAte
13. telEgraphy
14. tempEstuous
15. torrEntial
16. vulgArity

Words	Mnemonic Devices
_____	_____
	_____
	_____
_____	_____
	_____
	_____
_____	_____
	_____

Only you can provide answers for this exercise.

2. MEMORIZING

If such mnemonic devices cannot enable you to solve the problem of unstressed vowels in all the words that you actually misspell, then you may have to deal with the remaining ones by memorizing their spellings. The chances are that only a few such words remain in your personalized list of misspellings.

As you work on these remaining words, copy them in a special way so that the letter(s) causing you the trouble will stand out conspicuously while you work with the word. Thus if the *e* of *catEgory* is the culprit, capitalize, underline, or encircle that *e* in red—anything to burn that letter into your mind. You will not have to focus your attention upon that letter for long before that letter will be branded into your brain.

Or if your personalized list of misspellings is not up to date, you may use those procedures for gaining a mastery of these twenty frequently misspelled words, all of them fiends because of at least one unstressed vowel:

acceptable	difference	possible
acquaintance	discipline	prevalent
apparent	humor	privilege
comparative	independent	probably
consistent	permanent	repetition
decision	pleasant	separate
description		summary

3. INCREASING YOUR SENSE OF DOUBT

Though mnemonic devices and memorizing can help you greatly with the spelling of unstressed vowels, they cannot do the whole job. For example, they cannot help you with the spelling of new words—that is, words which you have never before spelled. Also, they cannot help you with words which you use so rarely that you have not yet memorized them or devised a mnemonic device for their spelling. So, even if these two earlier methods for dealing with the problem have been extremely useful, you will still have to rely at least part of the time upon your sense of doubt. Increasing your sense of doubt is therefore still important for you.

What you have already learned from this chapter has unquestionably increased your sense of doubt. Already you have seen how inconsistent, how unpredictable, how downright treacherous the spelling of these vowels is. It defies all rules, all reason.

Your sense of doubt will be further increased when you realize that these tricky spellings are just about everywhere in the language. They occur in just about every word with two or more syllables. On top of that, they occur in just about every position in those words: in prefixes, stems, and suffixes.

For instance, they are in the prefixes *de (declare)* and *di (divorce)*:

de	*di*
debate	digress
debauch	dilute
depress	diminish
demand	diploma
develop	divulge

In words like those, neither pronunciation nor meaning can give you a clue as to how the unstressed vowel is spelled.

The fiends are also lurking in the middle of words or stems, as in *catEgory, comparAtive, maintEnance, optImism, propAganda,* and *sepArate.*

And they are equally treacherous in suffixes. For example, look at them in these three groups of competing suffixes:

ant	*ent*
applicant	accident
defiant	competent
gallant	excellent
luxuriant	obedient
tolerant	reverent

able	ible
acceptable	accessible
excitable	flexible
incurable	incredible
passable	possible
respectable	susceptible

ar	er	ir
calendar	adviser	elixir
dollar	cloister	fakir
grammar	hunger	
hangar	loafer	
vulgar	swindler	

or	ur	yr
actor	murmur	martyr
clamor	sulfur	satyr
executor		
sponsor		
terror		

Then, just for fun, notice how *library, finery, sensory,* and *luxury* are spelled, with a *y* tacked on to the end of those suffixes. Finally, as a climax to it all, notice *laundry* and *sundry,* which have no vowel whatsoever before the *r.*

Such lists could be extended almost endlessly, but the words already given may be enough to demonstrate that the spelling of unstressed vowels is incredibly treacherous. You should be as suspicious of their spellings as you are of pink and purple dollar bills. SO, UNLESS YOU ARE ABSOLUTELY SURE OF THE SPELLING OF AN UNSTRESSED VOWEL, LOOK IT UP IN YOUR NEARBY DICTIONARY.

EXERCISE 5D

Put the needed vowel in the blank. Mark the "D" column if you are doubtful about that vowel.

	D
1. A terr __ ced field	____
2. An unusual privil __ ge	____
3. Cann __ bals enjoyed the missionary.	____
4. She has made consist __ nt progress.	____
5. Some Christians have been mart __ rs.	____

6. The airplane is in the hang ___ r.   ____

7. Some mushrooms are ed ___ ble.   /‾

8. Return this book to the libr ___ ry.   ___

9. Don't be so friv ___ lous.   ____

10. She will not d ___ vulge a secret.   ____

11. Consider the ev ___ dence before deciding.   ____

12. Her ac ___ demic progress   ____

13. A strange predic ___ ment

14. An exist ___ nce after life   ____

15. Put an excl ___ mation mark there.   ____

16. A question ___ ble belief   ____

17. Overcame all obst ___ cles   ____

18. A long-antic ___ pated day   ____

19. Became a brig ___ dier general   ____

20. The ord ___ nary routine   ____

For answers see box on page 49.

POSTTEST 5

Put the needed vowel in the blank. Mark the "D" column if you are doubtful about that vowel.

                                           D

1. Thirty-six fatal ___ ties   ____

2. The lux ___ ry of soft furs   ____

3. Insep ___ rable companions   ____

4. An incred ___ ble story   ____

5. A diff ___ cult assignment   ____

6. Their murm ___ r of approval   ____

7. No work in math ___ matics   ____

8. His persist ___ nt effort   ____

9. A new gramm ___ r book   ____

10. This fund ___ mental truth   ____

For answers see box on page 51.

6

OMITTED LETTERS

PRETEST 6

Put a letter, *if needed*, into each blank. If you are doubtful about your spelling of a word, mark the "D" column.

		D
1.	House of Represen __ atives	___
2.	His photographic mem __ ry	___
3.	Failed to reco __ nize her	___
4.	Huge quan __ ities of food	___
5.	A math __ matical problem	___
6.	Went to the lib __ ary	___
7.	Two choc __ late sundaes	___
8.	The cost of gover __ ment	___
9.	As reg __ larly as a clock	___
10.	The length __ ning shadows	___

For answers see box on page 53.

SILENT LETTERS AS OMITTED LETTERS

Because our spellings are often guided by our pronunciations, we often leave out letters which have become silent. Many sounds, once pronounced in English, are no longer pronounced, but the letters representing them have survived in our spelling. They are the ones most likely to be omitted when we spell.

Sounds have been dropping out of English words for more than a thousand years—for at least as long as the oldest records of the language can offer evidence. Furthermore, they are still dropping out (contrast *they've* with *they have*) and will probably continue to drop out for as long as the language lasts.

48

When these sounds gradually disappear from the language, they tend to go first in one dialect, then in a second dialect, a third ... and so on until they have disappeared from all the dialects in the language. Right now some sounds have dropped out of certain dialects but not out of other dialects. That is why the dialect which you happen to speak may influence the answers that you gave on the pretest for this chapter—why misspellings that seem strange to one person may seem almost inevitable to another person, who speaks a different dialect of English.

Despite such differences in dialect, the dropouts causing the biggest problems in English spelling belong to three groups, which may now be considered one at a time.

UNSTRESSED VOWELS AS DROPOUTS

In the previous chapter you saw how vowels, when they became unstressed in earlier centuries, tended to lose their distinctive sounds to become an indistinct "uh" or *i*. That is the first step in a two-step process by which they gradually disappear completely and thus become silent.

That process may again be illustrated by *victorious, victory,* and *victery,* plus a fourth form of the word: *victry.* In *victorious* the *o* is still stressed and therefore comes through loud and clear as an "oh" sound.

ANSWERS, EXERCISE 5D

1. terrAced	11. evIdence
2. privilEge	12. acAdemic
3. cannIbals	13. predicAment
4. consistEnt	14. existEnce
5. martYrs	15. exclAmation
6. hangAr	16. questionAble
7. edIble	17. obstAcles
8. librAry	18. anticIpated
9. frivOlous	19. brigAdier
10. dIvulge	20. ordInary

If all your spellings were correct or if all your misspellings were marked doubtful, go on the next chapter. If not, review this chapter before taking the posttest.

In *victory* it was once stressed, too, and therefore had an unmistakable "oh" sound. But a loss of stress changed "oh" to "uh"—a reason why the word is now sometimes misspelled as *victery* instead of *victory*. A further loss of stress is still going on, causing the faint "uh" to disappear. That is why the word is now sometimes misspelled as *victry*, with no vowel at all between the *t* and the *r*. (If no vowel occurs in the pronunciation there, leaving one out in the spelling there is a strong temptation—the chief reason for that particular misspelling.)

Here are some other vowels which are becoming silent or have already become silent and therefore cause trouble in spelling:

A	boundAry, laborAtory, liAble, literAture, miniAture, NiagAra, temperAment, temperAture
E	considErable, diffErent, delivEry, lengthEning, mathEmatics, misEry, scenEry
I	crimInal, defInite, defInition, famIly, simIlar
O	chocOlate, frivOlous, histOry, ignOrant, memOry, sophOmore
U	accUracy, casUalties, continUous, luxUry, regUlar

Say those words aloud to discover whether the capitalized letters are silent in your speech. If they are, repeat those words aloud, marking the silent letters with a dot, and then review those words until you are keenly aware of the silent letters lurking in them, ready to trap you into a misspelling.

CONSONANTS AS DROPOUTS

Consonants become silent not so much through a loss of stress as through the influence of nearby sounds. The two expressions "used car" and "used to live there" are examples of how nearby sounds can influence each other. When you say "used car," you pronounce the *d* in *used;* but when you say "used to live there," you almost certainly do not pronounce that *d*. Actually say those two expressions aloud, listening for the *d,* and you will almost certainly hear it only in the first of those expressions. For most people, it has become silent in the second. That is why *used to* is so often misspelled as *use to,* without the *d*. After all, if it is not pronounced, why spell it?

Why does *d* tend to disappear from *u̇sed to?* It is because of the influence of a nearby sound, the *t* of *to*. Those two sounds, *d* and *t,* are pronounced in almost exactly the same way, with lips and tongue in exactly the same positions. Paying close attention to what you do with your lips and tongue, pronounce first one, *"d-d-d-d,"* and then the other, "*t-t-t-*." the only difference in the pronunciation of them is this: your vocal cords, near your Adam's apple, are vibrating when you say *d*, but not when you say *t*.

Now consider *used to* again. Those similar sounds are right next to each other in that expression. So you must—if you pronounce all the letters there—manipulate your lips and tongue in the same way twice, first with your vocal cords vibrating (for the *d*) and then with your vocal cords not vibrating (for the *t*)—all this in a split second. What most people do in this complicated situation is to simplify it: they put lips and tongue in the proper positions only once, and they do not bother to rev up the vocal cords during that instant. As a result, they pronounce *used to* as though it were spelled *use to* and then, understandably, they begin to misspell it as *use to,* with the *d* omitted. (The *d* remains in *used car* because that combination of sounds does not require the double-lipping and the double-tonguing that *used to* does.)

Just as a *d* sound tends to disappear before a *t* sound, so certain other consonants tend to disappear through the influence of other nearby sounds. In the tabulation below are seven consonants that are often silenced by nearby sounds and that are, as a result, overlooked in spelling:

C	ACquaint, aCquiescent, aCquire, aCquit, arCtic, antarCtic, fasCinate
D	(after *n*) anD, canDidate, granDfather, grinDstone, hanDsome, lanDlord, sanDman
	(before *t*) useD to, supposeD to, hoped to
G	recoGnize
N	(next to *m*) columN, condemN, enviroNment, goverNment
P	(after *m*) consumPtion, emPty, promPt, pumPkin, temPt
R	(nearby *r*) FebRuary, libRary, suRprise

T   (after *f*) ofTen, sofTen

           (after *n*) authenTic, idenTical, quanTity, represenTative, ten-Tative

           (after *p*) accepT, attempT, contempT, excepT, kepT, slepT, swepT, wepT

           (after *s*) chesTnut, fasTen, husTle, lisTen, nesTle, thisTle, tresTle, whisTle, wresTle

Are those seven consonants silent in your pronunciation of those words? To find out, say those words aloud, paying attention to your pronunciation of the capitalized letters. Put a dot under the capitalized letters which are silent for you, and then review the dotted words until you are fully aware of the silent consonants in them.

"FOREIGN" LETTERS AS DROPOUTS

Foreign languages have foreign sounds—that is, sounds which do not occur in English. So when a foreign word enters English, it often brings with it a letter to represent that sound, a letter which speakers of English do not pronounce. Then, when speakers of English try to spell the word, they are likely to leave out the "foreign" letter.

The word *Buddha,* from Sanskrit, illustrates what happens. English has only one *d* sound, but Sanskrit has two: one spelled *d,* and the other spelled *dh.* Both of those sounds occurred in that word, and both were therefore included in its spelling: *Buddha.* But speakers of English are often tempted to misspell it as *Budda* or even *Buda*—the way they pronounce the word.

Here are some other imported words with silent letters that are easy to overlook.

H   dHow, maH-jongG, rHapsody, rHeostat, rHetoric, rHeumatism, rHubarb, rHyme, rHthym

M   Mnemonics

P   Pfennig, Pneumatic, Pneumonia, Pseudonym, Psychedelic, Psychic, Psychology.

Most of those imported silent letters lead to spellings that are so strange, so downright freakish, that, once they have been noticed, they are easy to remember. How can you, after once taking a really good look at the spelling of *mah-jongg,* ever forget it?

Just as foreign languages have foreign sounds, so do they have foreign spellings—that is, strange spellings for sounds that are in English as well as in the foreign language. The French word *chateau* is an example of a word, now in the English, which retains its foreign spelling. If it were a native word, it would probably be spelled *shato*. In the French system of spelling, however, the sound of *sh* (as in *shout*) is spelled *ch*, and the sound of *o* (as in *go*) is spelled *eau*. Thus the French spelling has seven letters where the English spelling would have only five—a potential dropping out of two letters.

The temptation to omit letters from imported words is strong, not only because the foreign words may have sounds which are not in English, but also because foreign spellings may include letters which are not needed in native spellings.

SYLLABLES AS DROPOUTS

Just as individual letters are sometimes left out of words, so are whole syllables. That sometimes happens with *accidentally*, when it is misspelled as *accidently*, without the *al*. In the same way, *incidentally* is sometimes misspelled as *incidently*; *functionally*, as *functionly*; and so for other words where the syllable *al* is omitted. Think of that syllable of being a fellow named *Al*, and you may be less likely to leave him out of these words: *accidentally*, *incidentally*, and *functionally*.

Though *Al* belongs in *accidentally*, he does not belong in *evidently*. Why? *Evident* is an adjective, and it becomes an adverb as soon as *ly* is added on to it. But *accident* is not an adjective—instead, it is a noun. Adding *al* to the noun converts it into an adjective, *accidental*; and adding *ly* to that adjective converts it into an adverb: *accidentally*. What *Al* does, you see, is to change nouns into adjectives, and then *ly* can change those adjectives into adverbs.

Like *evident* (and therefore requiring no *al* to form an adverb) are

ANSWERS, PRETEST 6

1. RepresenTatives
2. memOry
3. recoGnize
4. quanTities
5. mathEmatical
6. libRary
7. chocOlate
8. goverNment
9. regUlarly
10. lengthEning

If you made no mistakes here or marked your mistakes as doubtful spellings, go on to the next chapter. If not, study this chapter.

confident, frequent, recent, and numerous other such words. Only *ly* is needed to transform these adjectives into adverbs: *confidently, frequently,* and *recently.* But *ally,* with *Al* included, is needed to transform the nouns *accident, incident,* and *function* into the adverbs *accidentally, incidentally,* and *functionally.*

Even a few adjectives—those ending in *ic*—require *ally* to form adverbs: *basic–basically, psychopathic–psychopathically,* and *systematic–systematically.* Then, to make English spelling still more interesting, there is an exception to the *ic* rule: *publicly.*

Below are words frequently misspelled because needed letters are left out. Next to each word is a comment or a mnemonic device intended to help you to remember the proper spelling of the word. Study the spellings and the comments.

NOTE: Some of the following words are pronounced in different ways in different regions. As a result, some of the following comments may seem strange to speakers of certain dialects, but be genuinely helpful to speakers of other dialects. Use whichever comments seem helpful to you personally, and be tolerant about the "strange" comments intended to help the speakers of dialects different from your own.

accidentALly	Don't accidentALly forget your friend AL.
accUrate	U (you) should be accUrate.
arCtic	The ArCtic is on the arC of the earth.
aspIrin	When ASPIRINg for comfort, take aspIrin.
attempT	Girls who say "attemp" don't tempT.
authenTic	Not *nick,* but *tick; t* is often silent after *n.*
boundAry	The boundAry of a stAte.
CanDidate	CanDidates should be canDid; *d* is often silent after *n.*
chocOlate	ChocOlate is like cocOa.
considErable	ConsidEr it; don't considRA it.
crimInals	Put IN in crimINals and criminals IN prison.
diffErent	The word is not *diff-runt,* but *diffEr-ent.*
enviroNment	If possible, get iroN in your enviroNment.
FebRuary	Say "BR-R-R" in FeBRuary.
goverNment	Nobody "govers" a country; somebody goverNs it.
hanDsome	HanDsome men have hanDs; *d* is often silent after *n.*
idenTical	Even denTs are the same in idenTical things; *t* is often silent after *n.*
incidentALly	Don't forget your old friend AL.
lengthEning	To lengthEn, put something "in" it.
liAble	LiAble has three syllables; it does not rhyme with *Bible.*
literAture	Good students get an "A" in literAture.

mathEmatics	Note THE in maTHEmatics.
miniAture	MiniAture rhymes, almost, with "many a tour"; both have four syllables: min-i-A-ture.
morTgage	Earlier meant "death pledge." Note the *t* in such "death" words as *morTal* and *morTality*.
promptTly	Timed to a "t"; *t* is often silent after *p*.
quanTity	The quanTiTy of *t*'s in the word *quanTiTy* is two. Also, *t* is often silent after *n*.
recoGnize	CoGs move in your head when you recoGnize or become COGnizant again.
regUlar	To make regUlar is to regUlate.
represenTative	RepresenTatives are not "sin" to Congress, but are "senT" there.
sevEral	*Sev* is not a word, but *sevEr* is. *SevEr* is evEr a word, and the *al* makes it an adjective.
sophOmore	*SophOmore* is as long as *semaphOre:* three syllables.
supposeD to	*SupposeD to* has the *d* for the same reason that *wanteD to* and *wisheD to* do—to show past tense.
temperAment	Good students get an "A" in temperAment as well as in literAture.
temperAture	A good temperAture is temperAte.
useD to	A useD car useD to be owned by somebody else. The word is spelled the same in both expressions.

EXERCISE 6

If needed, put a letter into each blank. If you are doubtful about your spelling of a word, mark the "D" column.

D

1. The northern bound __ ry   ____

2. A can __ idate for office   ____

3. Mild temper __ ture in Hawaii   ____

4. Saw a famil __ ar face   ____

5. Some battles cas __ alties   ____

6. Attemp __ the impossible   ____

7. Gover __ ment of the people   ____

8. A diff __ rent plan   ____

9. The mis __ ry of defeat   ____

10. Pay off the mor __ gage   ____

11. Consid ___ rable effort   ___

12. An acc ___ rate measure   ___

13. His crim ___ nal tendencies   ___

14. A complete su ___ prise   ___

15. A statue of Budd ___ a   ___

16. An antar ___ tic expedition   ___

17. A sim ___ lar policy   ___

18. Russian liter ___ ture   ___

19. A ___ quired a good tan   ___

20. Magnificent scen ___ ry   ___

For answers see box on page 59.

POSTTEST 6

If needed, put a letter into each blank. If you are doubtful about a spelling, mark the "D" column.

                                                         D

1. Heredity or enviro ___ ment   ___

2. Made ten ___ ative plans   ___

3. The next ar ___ tic expedition   ___

4. As a soph ___ more in college   ___

5. Late in Feb ___ uary   ___

6. Iden ___ ical twins   ___

7. A new a ___ quaintance   ___

8. Suppose ___ to be here   ___

9. A fas ___ inating story   ___

10. Some r ___ ubarb pie   ___

For answers see box on page 61.

7

ADDED LETTERS

If needed, put a letter into each blank. If you are doubtful about a spelling, mark the "D" column.

		D
1.	Director of ath __ letics	___
2.	A black umb __ rella	___
3.	Rememb __ rance of old times	___
4.	Like a drown __ ed rat	___
5.	His griev __ ous error	___
6.	A prepost __ rous lie	___
7.	The op __ inion of experts	___
8.	Im __ agine my excitement!	___
9.	An occas __ ion for joy	___
10.	A hind __ rance to success	___

For answers see box on page 63.

Just as some misspellings are caused by leaving out a needed letter, so are others caused by adding unneeded ones. These surplus letters are most often the result of unjustified doubling, of the influence of another form of the word, of mispronunciation, or of irregular spellings.

UNJUSTIFIED DOUBLING

Often that unneeded letter is the result of improper doubling—say, the use of a double *f* where only one *f* is correct. Frequently misspelled in that way are *professor* and *profession*. The *fess* in those words is historically the same as the one in the word *confess* and in the expression

57

"'fess up." Doubling the *f* in *professor* and *profession* is therefore like writing *conFFess* and "'FFess up"—an obvious error. From now on, doubling the *f* in *professor* and *profession* may be an error that is just as obvious to you.

An unjustified doubling of *f* in *define, definite,* and *definition* is another frequent error. You would never think of spelling *fine* as *FFine* or *finite* as *FFinite.* Those spellings, you recognize, are ridiculous. Just as ridiculous are the spellings of *define, definite,* and *definition* with unjustified doublings.

Four common words—*amount, coming, imagine,* and *omit*—are often misspelled because the *m* is unjustifiably doubled. Two—*opinion* and *operate*—are frequently and unfortunately given an extra *p. Occasion* often gets an extra *s; shining* an extra *n,* and *careful* and *until* an extra *l.* Those last two spellings suggest that when words like *full* and *till,* with a double *l,* become suffixes, they drop an *l;* but, as if to keep English spelling complicated, that rule does not work with *fulfill,* where the stem instead of the suffix drops the *l.* Except in *fulfill,* a deviant spelling, the rule does work.*

INFLUENCE OF OTHER FORMS

Most other misspellings caused by extra letters are due to the influence of one form of a word upon another form of the same word. Because the verb *exclaim* contains *ai,* there is the temptation to put *ai* in the noun *exclamation,* misspelling it as *exclaimation.* In the same way, the verb *explain* tempts us to misspell the noun *explanation* by putting an unneeded *i* in it, misspelling it as *explaination.* Likewise, *repeat* may cause *repetition* to be misspelled as *repeatition.* And so for other similar words, where the stress shifts from one syllable to another as the form of the word changes. That explains why *maintain,* when transformed into a noun, becomes *maintenance,* not *maintainance.*

Extra letters sometimes sneak into a spelling even when there is no shift in stress. Thus, with no change in stress, *forty* is sometimes misspelled as *foUrty,* through the influence of *four;* and *ninth* is similarly misspelled as *ninEth* through the influence of *ninE,* just as *width* is misspelled as *widEth* through the influence of *widE.*

Other intrusive letters include a *u* in the misspelling of *among* as *amoung,* no doubt influenced by the *u* in the rhyming word *young.* The extra *p* in the misspelling of *opinion* as *opPinion* and of *operation* as *opPeration* is no doubt influenced by many words like *oppose,* which

---

Fulfil is a spelling that competes with *fulfill.* For a discussion of competing spellings, see Chapter 18.

have a double *p* after the initial *o*. In somewhat the same way, the frequent misspelling of *speech* as *speAch* may be influenced by the correct spelling of *speak,* where the *a* properly occurs; and the misspelling of *writer* as *writter* may be influenced by the correct spelling of *written,* which has the double *t*.

MISPRONUNCIATION

In all those words the excrescent letters slipped into the spelling through the influence of some other spelling; they may also sneak in as a result of a mispronunciation of a word. Thus if *across* is mispronounced with a *t* at the end, the word may be misspelled as *acrosT.* In the same way, other mispronunciations may lead to the misspelling of *area* as *areaR, athlete* as *athAlete, athletics* as *athAletics, idea* as *ideaR, drowned* as *drownDed,* and *height* as *heightH.* By saying those words aloud, you will discover whether or not you pronounce the letters capitalized above. If you do, your mispronunciation of them is almost certain to trap you into misspelling them. So listen to your pronunciation of them now, before reading on.

ANSWERS, EXERCISE 6

1. boundAry	11. considErable
2. canDidate	12. accUrate
3. temperAture	13. crimInal
4. famillar	14. suRprise
5. casUalties	15. BuddHa
6. attempT	16. antarCtic
7. goverNment	17. simIlar
8. diffErent	18. literAture
9. misEry	19. aCquired
10. morTgage	20. scenEry

If you made no mistakes or marked all your misspellings as doubtful, go on to the next chapter. If not, review this chapter before taking the posttest.

IRREGULAR SPELLINGS

Nine other words are so frequently misspelled, because an extra letter is inserted into them, that they are disastrous for many students. Because *disastrous* itself is one of these words, the nine may be called the "disastrous" group. The villainous letter which sneaks into these words is an *e* before the *r*, and it usually gets in through the influence of the spelling of another form of the word. For example, *disastEr* has that *e*, but *disastrous* most emphatically does not have it. To put an *e* before the *r* in *disastrous* is to misspell the word, and the same is true of these other eight words in the group: *entrance, hindrance, lustrous, monstrous, remembrance, suffrage, umbrella,* and *wondrous*.

* * *

In summary, superfluous letters are most often caused by unjustified doubling, as in *define* and *professor;* by the influence of the spelling of another form of a word, as in *exclamation* and *explanation;* by mispronunciations, as in *across* and *athletics;* and by the nine "disastrous" words.

Below are some words frequently misspelled because extra letters are added to them. Next to each word is a comment or a mnemonic device intended to help you to remember the correct spelling of the word. Study the spellings and the comments.

Word	Comment
across	No teacher is ever suited to a *t* by a *t* in *across*.
among	*Among* is an old word, with just an *o* in it, not a young word, with an *ou* in it.
amount	*Amount* is pronounced like "a mount," without a double *m*.
area	An area is never a rear.
athletics	"AthA" is no good in athletics.
coming	*Come* has only one *m*, and so does *coming*. Unjustified doubling.
define	FF is no better in *define* than in *fine*. Unjustified doubling.
disastrous	*Astrology* has no *e*, and neither does *disastrous*, which earlier meant "unfavorable stars." A "disastrous" word to spell.
drowned	*Drown* rhymes with *down*, not *grounD*. A pilot may be grounDed, but a swimmer can never be drownDed.
entrance	An entrance, meaning "a door," may entrance, meaning "enrapture." The two words are spelled the same, without an *e* before the *r*. A "disastrous" word.

Word	Comment
exclamation	To get an exclamation, take *i* out of *exclaim*.
explanation	To get an explanation, take *i* out of *explain*.
forty	The first of *forty* is pronounced (and spelled) more like *for* than *four*.
fulfill	This word has a deviant spelling: a double *l* in the suffix but a single *l* in the stem. Its spelling is therefore one to be especially doubtful about, unless you memorize it, preferably right now.
height	*Height* rhymes with *kite*.
hindrance	A hindrance is a hurdle, with no *e* before the *r*. A "disastrous" word.
idea	*Idea* does not rhyme with *dear*.
imagine	Images fill your imagination when you imagine. Unjustified doubling.
lustrous	*Lustrous* rhymes with *truss*, and neither has an *e* before the *r*. A "disastrous" word.
maintenance	The second syllables of *maintenance* and *maintain* are not pronounced alike and therefore are not spelled alike. A "saving of face" is a "maintEnance of countEnance."
monstrous	That which is monstrous can be disastrous, especially with an *e*.
ninth	Know ye that no *e* is in *ninth*.
occasion	Unjustified doubling of *s*.
omit	Unjustified doubling of *m*.
operate	Just one *p*, please. Unjustified doubling.
opinion	Again, just one *p*, please.
professor	A second *f* brings an "F" on spelling.
remembrance	A remembrance is somewhere in a membrane of your brain, not in a membErane of your bErain. A "disastrous" word.
repetition	Most of *repetition* rhymes with *competition*—and is spelled like it.

Word	Comment
shining	Don't confuse shining a light with shinning up a tree. Unjustified doubling.
speech	In spelling, a speech resembles a screech.
suffrage	The *r* in this word goes with *rage*, not *suffer*. A "disastrous" word.
umbrella	An unbreakable umbrella is better than an un-bEreakable umbErella. A "disastrous" word.
until	A double *l* is an *l* of a way to spell *until*.
wondrous	An amazing thing about *wondrous* is that it contains no *e*. A "disastrous" word.
writing	*Writing*, with one *t* is not pronounced like *written*, with two, and therefore is not spelled like it. Unjustified doubling.

EXERCISE 7

If needed, put a letter into each blank. If you are doubtful about a spelling, mark the "D" column.

                                                         D

1. A clear expla __ nation   ____
2. In the op __ erating room   ____
3. An all-around ath __ lete   ____
4. This lust __ rous diamond   ____
5. Just across __ the street   ____
6. A marvelous idea __   ____
7. Now a prof __ essor at Princeton   ____
8. The wond __ rous news   ____
9. A careful __ examination   ____
10. About fo __ rty people   ____
11. An annoying hind __ rance   ____
12. That famous writ __ er   ____
13. His def __ inition of "zygoma"   ____
14. To om __ it flowers   ____
15. The height __ of folly   ____
16 A monst __ rous mistake   ____

17. Wait until __ later   ___

18. Amo __ ng the last to leave   ___

19. The racer who was nin __ th   ___

20. "From sea to shin __ ing sea"   ___

For answers see box on page 65.

POSTTEST 7

If needed, put a letter in each blank. If you are doubtful about a spelling, mark the "D" column.

                                            D

1. A disast __ rous fire   ___

2. Careful __ attention   ___

3. Just a small am __ ount   ___

4. An occas __ ion to celebrate   ___

5. Spread ac __ ross the prairie   ___

6. The blighted area __   ___

7. A prof __ essional opinion   ___

8. Skill in ath __ letics   ___

9. At the height __ of his fame   ___

10. Voted for women's suff __ rage   ___

For answers see box on page 67.

For answers see box on page 65.

For answers see box on page 67.

ANSWERS, PRETEST 7

Only one letter needed to be added: the *e* in *prepostErous*, 6.

8

IDENTICAL PRONUNCIATIONS

PRETEST 8

Two or more words are in parentheses in the following sentences. Underline the proper word. If you are doubtful about your choice, mark the "D" space.

D

1. We have (all ready, already) seen that show. ____
2. (Its, It's) your move now. ____
3. We bought linen (stationary, stationery). ____
4. His (principal, principle) worries are financial. ____
5. Don't talk (to, too, two) loud. ____
6. We (maybe, may be) there soon. ____
7. Use a (capital, capitol) letter. ____
8. (Their, There, They're) is no trouble yet. ____
9. Many (emigrants, immigrants) entered the country. ____
10. That was sent (to, too, two) him today. ____

For answers see box on page 69.

CARELESS CONFUSIONS

When two or more words are pronounced the same, as *there* and *their* are, we often substitute one for the other, thus becoming guilty of a misspelling. Often these substitutions are caused not by ignorance of the meanings of the two words but by sheer carelessness. In a flurry of fast writing, we put down a word which sounds right, but do not bother to notice whether it is spelled right. Even when rereading our work, searching for errors, we are especially likely to overlook a misspelling that "sounds right." Their correct pronunciation often conceals their incorrect spelling.

Such careless spellings of words with identical pronunciations are exceedingly common. Indeed, according to an extensive study of misspellings by college students, the most common of all possible misspellings involved the confusion of *there, their,* and *they're.* These college students must surely have known the difference in the meanings of those three expressions, but they carelessly substituted one expression for another—and then never noticed the difference.

In the same study of misspellings in college, the mistake which ranked second in frequency involved another group of three words with identical pronunciations; *too, two,* and *to.* Again the careless substitution of one of those words for another must be the explanation for those misspellings, for surely any college student can explain the differences in meaning among those words.

And carelessness, not ignorance, must also be responsible for the frequent misspelling of two other words, *its* and *it's*—a pair ranking seventeenth in the list of more than three hundred words most often misspelled. At any rate, carelessness (a personal rather than a verbal problem, please notice) must be responsible for most substitutions of *it's,* with the apostrophe, for *its,* without the apostrophe. If carelessness is not responsible, then there are college students who do not know a fundamental rule about English: no apostrophes with possessive pronouns, just with possessive nouns. The possessive pronouns ending in *s* include *yours, his, hers, its, ours,* and *theirs*—and not one of them, notice, contains an apostrophe. Only nouns include apostrophes in their possessive forms—not pronouns. (The association of apostrophes with possession may be a secondary cause of the substitution of *it's* for *its,* but the primary cause must be just plain carelessness.)

Because the groups of words represented by *there, too,* and *its* accounted for almost a thousand misspellings in a sampling of college writing, the careless substitution of one word for another with an identical pronunciation must be regarded as a major cause of misspelling. These facts also suggest—strongly—that a well-developed sense of doubt must be especially sensitive to words with identical pronunciations. Because their pronunciation tends to distract from their spelling, these words are something to be very suspicious about. They are, in effect, mistake-prone.

IGNORANT CONFUSIONS

Though the confusion of *there* with *their* must be caused by carelessness, the confusion of *complement* and *compliment* may be caused by ignorance—by a lack of knowledge about how the meanings of those two words differ from each other. That confusion, too, can lead to misspellings: to the improper substitution of one word (or spelling) for the other. That is why, in the remainder of this chapter, consideration will be given to pairs of words which may be confused, not only by carelessness, but also by ignorance.

Because the words dealt with here are pronounced exactly the same, their pronunciation is no clue at all to their spelling. If there is a clue to their spelling, it must be found, instead, in their meaning. That is why, in the following tabulation of some of the most common of these words, a separate column has been set aside for the basic meanings of the words and why meanings are also often referred to in the "Comment" column, where other aids to spelling are provided.

Word	Meaning	Comment
all ready	totally prepared	Compare "Dinner is all ready" and "They are all ready for dinner" with "They have already eaten dinner."
already	by now	*All ready* may be split by an intervening word; *already* cannot be so split. Compare "They are all ready to go" with "They all are ready to go." Then compare "They are already there" with "They al are ready there"—an impossibility in English.
		The two expressions can be used in a single sentence: "They are already (by now) all ready (totally prepared) to go."

Word	Meaning	Comment
all together	everybody together	Compare "Now, all together, pull" with "Now, all pull together." The two words may be split by an intervening word. But *altogether* cannot be split, any more than *wholly* can. "You're altogether wrong" cannot be written as "You're al wrong together."
altogether	wholly	
altar	a place of worship	Associate the "A" word with *mArriAge, rAbbi, BAptist, prAy, sAcred.*
alter	change	Notice that the vowels *a* and *e* are in the "AltEr," which means "chAngE."
capital	chief	The "O" word refers only to the building, which usually has a dOme. Associate *capitOl* with *dOme.* Use the "A" word, *capitAl,* unless you are referring to the domed building itself.
capitol	the building	
complement	to complete; that which completes	The "E" word complEtes. the "I" word refers to things that I lIke: *praIse, gIfts,* other *nIce thIngs.*
compliment	to praise; that which praises	Associate *complEment* with *supplEment;* associate *complIment* with *gifts* and *kIndness.*

Word	Meaning	Comment
emigrant	a person who goes OUT of a country	An Emigrant from Germany may be an Immigrant INto the United States.
immigrant	a person who comes INto a country	Associate the "E" word with *Exit, Expel, Emit, Erase.* Associate the "I" word with *In, Into.* Also associate *Emigrant* with *Export* and *Immigrant* with *Import.*
eminent	OUTstanding, high, lofty	The *e* is from *ex,* meaning "out," as in *exit.*
imminent	IMpending, about to happen	What is imminent is threatening, but what is eminent is looked up to, usually admired.
forth	forward	Associate the U of *foUrth* with the U of *nUmber.* The word *fOrth,* which has no U, has nothing to do with numbers.
fourth	4th	
its	belongs to it (possessive pronoun)	Possessive pronouns like *hers, his, its, theirs, whose,* and *yours* never have apostrophes. With pronouns similar to these, the apostrophe is a signal of a contraction, not of possession. Thus *it's* means "it is," and *its* means "possessed by it." NOTE: "It's (it is) its (possessed by it) own fault."
it's	it is (contraction)	
maybe	perhaps (adverb)	*Maybe* and *perhaps* are interchangeable. Compare "Maybe I'll go" with "Perhaps I'll go." But *may be* and *perhaps* are not interchangeable. Compare "I may be late" with "I perhaps late."
may be	might be (verb)	

Word	Meaning	Comment
principal	primary	Both *principle* and *rule* end in *le*, and both mean approximately the same thing. The best thing to do here is to use the "E" word if talking about a rulE and the "A" word if talking about Anything else.
principle	a rule	
stationary	standing still (adjective)	That which stAnds is stationAry. But *shEEts, EnvElopEs,* and *lEttErs* are stationEry.
stationery	writing materials (noun)	
their	belonging to them	*ThEIr* involves possession. So does *hEIr. ThErE* involves place. So do *hErE* and *whErE.* Associate *tHEIR* with *HEIR* and *tHERE* with *wHERE.* NOTE: "They're (these people are) there (at that place) near their (belonging to them) home."
there	at that place	
they're	they are (contraction)	
to	toward (preposition)	He went to town (noun after *to*).

Word	Meaning	Comment
to	(sign of infinitive)	He wants to buy a car (verb after *to*)
too	also; excessive (adverb)	He went, too. This was too much for her. *Too*, which means "excessive" has more *o*'s than any other word pronounced like it.
two	2 (adjective, number)	Associate *two*, which has the *w*, with *twice*, *twins*, and *twenty*, which also have *w*'s. NOTE: "The two parents, too, went to town to shop."
whose	belongs to whom (possessive pronoun)	Remember that possessive pronouns, like *hers*, *his*, *its*, *theirs*, *whose*, and *yours*, never have apostrophes. With pronouns similar to these, the apostrophe is a signal of contraction, not of possession. Thus *who's* means "who is," and *whose* means "possessed by whom." NOTE: "Who's (who is) sure whose (belongs to whom) hat this is?"
who's	who is (contraction)	
your	belongs to you (possessive pronoun)	Possessive personal pronouns, you recall, have no apostrophes.
you're	you are (contraction)	Personal pronouns with apostrophes are contractions. NOTE: "You're your worst enemy."

After you have studied the words tabulated above, do the following exercise.

EXERCISE 8

Two or more words are in parentheses in the sentences below. Underline the proper word. If you are doubtful about your choice, mark the "D" space.

                                                                              D

1. (Whose, Who's) move is it now?   ____

2. This is (your, you're) fault.   ____

3. The seasick passengers lost (there, their, they're) dinner.   ____

4. Our guests are (all ready, already) to go now.   ____

5. The preacher moved to the (altar, alter).   ____

6. Sue is (all together, altogether) charming.   ____

7. A (capital, capitol) is a building where the legislature meets.   ____

8. He was a man of high (principals, principles). ____

9. (Whose, Who's) the new pitcher?   ____

10. I have a (complement, compliment) from Leslie for you.   ____

11. Her grandfather (emigrated, immigrated) from Germany.   ____

12. (Its, It's) raining outside.   ____

13. Her house resembles a (manner, manor).   ____

14. You need a (capital, capitol) letter there.   ____

15. The destroyer did not have its full (complement, compliment) of men.   ____

16. You should not go (to, too, two) the races so often.   ____

17. This (may be, maybe) your last chance.   ____

18. Then a volunteer stepped (forth, fourth).   ____

19. Snow survived the thaw here and (their, there). ____

20. You may earn 6 percent interest on your (principal, principle) here.   ____

For answers see box on page 73.

POSTTEST 8

Two or more words are in parentheses in the sentences below. Underline the proper word. If you are doubtful about your choice, mark the "D" space.

D

1. (Your, You're) my best friend. ____

2. My horse came in (forth, fourth). ____

3. This is a (complementary, complimentary) copy. ____

4. Let's (altar, alter) the dress now. ____

5. The salt lost (its, it's) savor. ____

6. The locomotive stood (stationary, stationery). ____

7. (Whose, Who's) going with me? ____

8. (Maybe, May be) you are right. ____

9. That hat is (all together, altogether) captivating. ____

10. Albany is the (capital, capitol) of New York. ____

For answers see box on page 75.

9

SIMILAR PRONUNCIATIONS

Two words or spellings are in parentheses in the sentences below. Underline the correct one. If you are not sure about your choice, mark the "D" space.

D

1. The new model will (supercede, supersede) the old one. ___

2. He sent a bill for his legal (advice, advise). ___

3. Hopes should never (excede, exceed) abilities. ___

4. Don't (loose, lose) this key. ___

ANSWERS, EXERCISE 8

1. Whose	11. emigrated
2. your	12. It's
3. their	13. manor
4. all ready	14. capital
5. altar	15. complement
6. altogether	16. to
7. capitol	17. may be
8. principles	18. forth
9. Who's	19. there
10. compliment	20. principal

If you got all the answers right or marked all your mistakes as doubtful, go on to the next chapter. If not, review this chapter before taking the posttest.

5. Bankers (prophecy, prophesy) prosperity.   ____

6. Underline to (emphasise, emphasize).   ____

7. His hairline began to (recede, resede).   ____

8. How will that (affect, effect) his plans?   ____

9. To be popular, (bath, bathe) regularly.   ____

10. The crazy man wandered off into the (desert,   ____
    dessert) and starved to death.

For answers see box on page 77.

The words with similar pronunciations belong to four main groups, illustrated by (1) *safe–save*, (2) *secede–succeed*, (3) *decent–descent*, and (4) *prophecy–prophesy*.

THE "SAFE–SAVE" WORDS

Many words are like *safe* and *save* in that they have one spelling and pronunciation for their noun forms, and a slightly different one for their verb forms. The difference in pronunciation is a curious one, for the Verbs have a Voiced sound (notice the capital V's) at the very spot where the noUNs have an UNvoiced sound (notice the capital UN's). Even more curious, you can tell whether a sound is Voiced or UNvoiced (and thus whether one of these words is a Verb or a noUN) by placing your fingers on your Adam's apple while saying the words: you can feel your Adam's apple Vibrate with the sound in Voiced Verbs, but it does not vibrate, or is UNvibrating, with the sound in UNvoiced noUNs.

Try this yourself: Put your fingers on your Adam's apple, and say aloud for a few seconds the *f* sound *(f-f-f-f)*. Your Adam's apple does not vibrate, and you do not hear your voice—just a hissing sound. Next say aloud the *v* sound *(v-v-v-v)*. Now you can feel the vibration of your Adam's apple, and you can hear your voice, in addition to the hissing sound. The *v* is a voiced hissing sound, but the *f* is an unvoiced hissing sound. *Save* is a Voiced Verb; *safe*, an UNvoiced noUN (or adjective).

Almost half the consonants in the alphabet are involved in this principle of Voiced Verb and UNvoiced noUN. Here are some examples involving ten consonants:

Consonants	Voiced Verbs	UNvoiced noUNs
v-f	stri*v*e	stri*f*e
b-p	absor*b*	absor*p*tion
d-t	merchan*d*ising	merchan*t*
z-s	analy*z*e	analy*s*is
the-th	wrea*the*	wrea*th*

THE "SECEDE–SUCCEED" WORDS

All these words end with the sounds of "seed," which may be spelled in four different ways: *seed, sede, ceed,* or *cede.* The problem, not a difficult one to solve, is to decide which spelling of these sounds is to be used in a particular word.

The problem is easy to solve, for three of the four spellings are used in only a few words, and the fourth spelling is used in all the others:

> *seed* only in *seed* itself and in such combinations as *seedings* and *seedling.*
> *sede* only in *supersede.*
> *ceed* only in three words: *exceed, proceed,* and *succeed.*
> *cede* in all others, including *accede, antecede, cede, concede, intercede, PRECEDE, recede, retrocede,* and *secede.*

Reading this list only once more may solve this problem for you

THE "DECENT–DESCENT" WORDS

The *s* sound is spelled in at least three confusing ways: by *c* in *decent, sc* in *descent,* and *s* in *sent.* Whenever one of those spellings is improperly substituted for another, the result is, of course, a misspelling.

Such a substitution is especially likely where the *s* sound appears twice in the same words, but is spelled in two different ways, as in *license* and *science.* Another frequent substitution involves a use of *s* or *c* where both (or *sc*) are required, as in *adolescence, ascend, conscience, conscious, descend, discipline, fascinate, muscle, reminisce, scene,* and *science.* Because only one of those letters is sounded, only one is too often included in the spelling.

ANSWERS, POSTTEST 8

1. You're	6. stationary
2. fourth	7. Who's
3. complimentary	8. Maybe
4. alter	9. altogether
5. its	10. capital

Also troublesome are the suffixes *ence* and *ense*. Why should *absence, incidence,* and *magnificence* have a *c* where *expense, license,* and *suspense* have an *s*? Why should *council* have a *c* where *counsel* has an *s*? In addition, why should *fallacy* have a *c* where *fantasy* has an *s*? There are hidden historical reasons for these inconsistencies, but there are no reasons which are both obvious and logical. That is why an increased sense of doubt or memorizing may be the best way for dealing with them.

THE "PROPHECY–PROPHESY" WORDS

Some troublesome words with similar produnciations, such as *prophecy* and *prophesy,* must be considered a pair at a time, and their spelling must be mastered by a sense of doubt, by a mnemonic device, or by memorizing. Here are several of those rule-resisting pairs, with helpful hints in the "Comment" column:

Word	Meaning	Comment
accept	to receive	The *cept* means "to take." Because *ac* (assimilated* from *ad*) means "to," *accept* means "to take to."
except	to exclude	Because *ex* means "out," *except* means "to take out" or "to exclude." If "I accept a proposal," I take it to it. If "I accept all proposals *except* one," then I exclude one from acceptance.
affect	to change	*Affect* and *effect* have other meanings besides "to change" and "to cause," but these two meanings lead to most of the confusion between the words. The expression "cause and effect" will help you to associate "cause" with *effect. Effect* may be used where "to cause" may be substituted for it, as in "The tornado may effect (may 'cause,'
effect	to cause	

---

*Assimilation is explained in Chapter 13.

Word	Meaning	Comment
		not 'change') complete destruction." *Affect* is used where "to change" may be substituted for it, as in "The weather may affect (may 'change,' not 'cause') our plans."
amateur	a person who does something because he loves it	An amateur is a person; an armature, a thing. Other "person" words spelled with EUR are *chauffEUR* and *massEUR*. Other "thing" words spelled with URE are *dentURE, fixtURe, furnitURe*, and *overtURE*.
armature	a thing, a piece of equipment, as in a generator	Notice that ARMAment is a "thing," just as ARMAture is.
censer	a container for burning incense (noun)	Associate *inCENSE* with *CENSEr*.
censor	a person who cuts out what he thinks is immoral (noun, verb)	Associate *censOr* with *mOrality*.

ANSWERS, PRETEST 9

1. supersede
2. advice
3. exceed
4. lose
5. prophesy
6. emphasize
7. recede
8. affect
9. bathe
10. desert

If all your answers were right or if you marked your mistakes as doubtful, go on to the next chapter. If not, study this chapter first.

Word	Meaning	Comment
censure	to blame (verb)	Anybody who cenSUREs should be SURE of his facts. NOTE: The censOr cenSUREs the CENSEr for its bad odor.
choose	(present tense)	*Choose* rhymes with *ooze, booze,* and *snooze.*
chose	(past tense)	*Chose* rhymes with *rose, nose,* and *hose.* Compare "I once chose a rose" with "I now choose booze."
conscience	That which knows the difference between right and wrong (noun)	*NouN* and *coNscieNce* have two *n*'s; *conscious* and *adjective* do not. *ConSCIENCE* and *SCIENCE* are nouns; *consclOUS* and *glorIOUS* are adjectives.
conscious	being aware (adjective)	"He is always conscious of his conscience."
consul	a person	A *consul* is an official, often a nation's representative in a
council	a group of persons	foreign country. A *council* is a group of people or a meeting of that group. The group may
counsel	advice (or advise)	contain officials. *CounSEL* is what lawyers *SELL;* it is advice. "The council of consuls counseled caution."
desert	to leave (verb)	"The Soldier who deSerts gets punished." *Soldier* and *deSert* have only one *s*.
	a barren place (noun)	"The Sahara is a desert." *Sahara* and *deSert* have only one *s*.
	what is deserved (noun)	"He got his just deSerts." *DeServe* and this *deSert* have only one *s*.

Word	Meaning	Comment
dessert	the last course of a meal (noun)	"A Strawberry Shortcake is a good deSSert." *Strawberry Shortcake* and *deSSert* both have two *s*'s.
formally	in a formal manner	Associate the A in *formAlly* with the A in *pArty, mAnner, invitAtion.*
formerly	earlier	Associate the ERLY in *formERLY* with *EARLY.* An ex-wife is a former wife, not a formal wife.
loose	not tight (adjective)	Once there was a goose Whose feathers came loose.
lose	to misplace (verb)	She was afraid to use them For fear she might lose them.
material	something made of matter	This word, with AL, is the one that is ALmost ALways used.
matériel	equipment, especially military equipment	Since war is hell, *matériel* may appropriately be rhymed with *hell.* Both contain EL. NOTE; The material became matériel.
moral	involving right and wrong (adjective; *morals* is a noun)	Thirsty soldiers discovering a warehouse of wines are likely to have a greater improvement in morale than in morals. NOTE: ALE may improve the morALE of troops more than it will improve their morals.
morale	general attitude (noun)	
personal	belonging to a person (adjective)	*PersoNal*, with one N, may refer to only one person; but *persoNNel*, with more than one N, cannot refer to only one person.

Word	Meaning	Comment
personnel	a staff of people (noun and adjective)	Contrast "personal office" with "personnel office."
precede	to go in front of	*Precede* must have a noun after it as an object; *proceed* cannot have a noun after it as an object.
proceed	to go forward	Contrast "Women precede men" with "Proceed with your work."
prophecy	a prediction (noun)	The *c* in *prophecy* indicates a noun, as in *advice* and *device*. The *s* in *prophesy* indicates a verb, as in *advise* and *devise*.
prophesy	to predict (verb)	"Prophets prophesy, but their prophecies are seldom right."
quiet	silent, or nearly so	*Quiet* and *silent* are both pronounced in two syllables; *qui-et* and *si-lent*. But *quite* is pronounced in one syllable, just as *night* is.
quite	completely	Contrast the pronunciations of *quite noisy* and *quiet noisy*.
respectfully	full of respect	Associate *respectfully* with *full of respect*.
respectively	consecutively	Associate *respectively* with consecutively.
statue	a work of art	A statUe may be made of YOU, but a stature and a statute cannot be made of YOU.
stature	size	Associate the R of *statuRe* with the R of *laRge*.
statute	a law	Associate the T's of *sTaTe* with the extra T in *sTaTuTe*, because a sTaTe may pass sTaTuTes. NOTE: "A statue showed Lincoln, a man of large stature, signing a statute."

Word	Meaning	Comment
weather	rain, snow, etc.	Associate wEAther with clEAr or drEAry.
whether	if	"I don't know whether the weather will be clear or dreary tomorrow."

After studying this list carefully, do the next exercise.

EXERCISE 9

If needed, put a letter in the following blanks. If you are doubtful about your spelling, mark the "D" column.

D

1. Analy __ e the problem first.   ___
2. She wore a sheath __ dress.   ___
3. An atomic devi __ e was exploded there.   ___
4. The doctor cauteri __ ed the boil.   ___
5. They grie __ ed about her death.   ___
6. We began to breath __ more easily.   ___
7. We decided to moderni __ e the house.   ___
8. She said, "I loath __ you!"   ___
9. Cotton has great capacity for absor __ tion.   ___
10. Please excu __ e me for a moment.   ___
11. We will penali __ e all violators of the law.   ___
12. Gentlemen, sheath __ your swords.   ___
13. He refu __ ed to move an inch.   ___
14. Fragrant cens __ rs were burning in the temple.   ___
15. Finally, after much persuasion, he took a bath __ .   ___
16. Take my advi __ e and buy that stock.   ___
17. England nationali __ ed her railroads.   ___

18. The baby has begun to teeth __ .   ____

19. Write a descri __ tion of your home.   ____

20. Man ideali __ es the woman he loves.   ____

For answers see box on page 85.

POSTTEST 9

Two words or spellings are in parentheses in the sentences below. Underline the correct one. If you are not sure of your choice, mark the "D" space.

D

1. He (preceded, proceeded) with his lecture.   ____

2. In the park is a (statue, statute) of Lincoln.   ____

3. Be sure before you (criticise, criticize).   ____

4. They were (quiet, quite) excited about it.   ____

5. The football team refused to (concede, con-   ____
   ceed) the game.

6. Was he (conscience, conscious) then?   ____

7. Whom will you (chose, choose)?   ____

8. He will (succede, succeed) in his job.   ____

9. Apply for work at the (personal, personnel)   ____
   office.

10. Do you know (weather, whether) he is very   ____
    ill?

For answers see box on page 87.

10

IE or EI?

PRETEST 10

Put *ie* or *ei* in each blank. If you are doubtful about your choice, mark the "D" column.

	D			D
1. f __ rce	___	**6.** R __ lly	___
2. kal __ doscope	___	**7.** perc __ ve	___
3. forf __ t	___	**8.** caff __ ne	___
4. var __ gation	___	**9.** gr __ f	___
5. s __ smograph	___	**10.** s __ zure	___

For answers see box on page 89.

Words like *counterfeit, deceive,* and *deity* raise a question: Does *i* come before *e*? Or *e* before *i*?

A fresh study of about nine hundred words spelled with *ie* or *ei* shows that *i* comes before *e* in about six hundred words, but *e* before *i* in about three hundred. Thus *ie* is about twice as frequent as *ei*. A new bit of doggerel is intended to emphasize that *i*, more often than not, comes before *e*:

> Just as I always want to be before thee,
> So does *i* always want to be before *e*.

More accurately, *i* comes before *e* except when the two letters are pronounced as in the words in this grotesque sentence:

> The eight counterfeit steins deceived the deity.

Here the two letters are pronounced as long *a* in *eight,* as short *i* in *counterfeit,* as long *i* in *stein,* as long *e* in *deceived,* and as two separate sounds, in separate syllables, in *deity*—as long *e* in the first syllable and

83

as "uh" in the second. Thus use *ie* unless the two letters are pronounced as in *The eight counterfeit steins deceived the deity.*

THE "EIGHT" WORDS—WITH THE SOUND OF LONG A

When the two letters are pronounced with the sound of long **a,** *as in* **eight,** *the* **e** *comes before* **i.**

This rule has no known exceptions and applies to scores of words, including *beige, deign, freight, neighbor, rein, seine, surveillance, veil,* and *weight.*

THE "COUNTERFEIT" AND "STEIN" WORDS— WITH THE SOUNDS OF SHORT I AND LONG I

When the two letters have the sound of **i**—*short in* **counterfeit** *or long in* **stein**—*the* **e** *comes before the* **i** *unless the* **i** *sound is last in the shortest form of the word.*

Notice that the *i* sound is not last in *counterfeit,* where it is followed by a *t* sound, or in *stein,* where it is followed by an *n* sound. But the *i* sound is last in *menagerie* (note the *i* before the *e* there) and in *sty* (note the *i* before the *e* in *sties*). Thus when the two letters have an *i* sound, the crucial question is whether or not that sound is last in the shortest form of the word. If it is last, the spelling is *ie;* if it is not last, the spelling is *ei.*

Like *counterfeit*—with the sound of short *i* in a nonfinal position in the shortest form of the word—are *foreign, forfeit, sovereign, surfeit,* and many other words. Like *stein*—with the sound of long *i* in a nonfinal position in the shortest form of the word—are *eider* (duck), *Einstein, kaleidoscope, seismograph, sleight of hand,* and many other words.

For some dialects this rule has no known exceptions. But for the dialects where the *ie* of *bier, fierce,* and *cashier* is pronounced with the sound of short *i,* these words—and all others with the two letters just before an *r*—are exceptions. If you pronounce these *r* words with short *i,* then these words are exceptions for you. But if you pronounce these *r* words with long *e,* they are not exceptions to this rule; moreover, they then conform to the rule for the *"deceived"* words. Right now decide whether or not these *r* words are exceptions for you, and spell them accordingly in the future.

THE "DECEIVED" WORDS—WITH THE SOUND OF LONG E

When the two letters are pronounced with the sound of long **e,** *as in* **deceived,** *the* **e** *comes before the* **i** *only after* **c.**

Words with the two letters right after *c* include *ceiling, conceit, conceive, deceit, deceive, perceive,* and *receive.* These words, please notice, have the *e* before the *i.* But other words have the *i* before *e: achieve, belief, chief, niece, piece, siege,* and *yield.* As such examples show, the two letters have one order (*ei*) after *c;* the opposite (*ie*) when not after *c.*

But there are some exceptions to this rule. Four words, *sheik, seize, weir,* and *weird,* have the *e* before the *i* even when there is no preceding *c;* and so do many proper names, including *Reid* and *Sheila.* In addition, some words with *c* near the end have the *i* before *e,* even right after the *c,* as in *consistencies, frequencies, policies, specie,* and *species.* Perhaps this grotesque sentence will help you to remember these exceptions: *Sheila seized a species of sheik.*

Certain other words are exceptions in some dialects, but not in others. One group of these other possible exceptions is made up of such technical words as *caffeine, codeine,* and *protein.* And the other group

---

ANSWERS, EXERCISE 9

1.	analyze	11.	penalize
2.	sheath	12.	sheathe
3.	device	13.	refused
4.	cauterized	14.	censers
5.	grieved	15.	bath
6.	breathe	16.	advice
7.	modernize	17.	nationalized
8.	loathe	18.	teethe
9.	absorption	19.	description
10.	excuse	20.	idealizes

If all your answers are right or if the incorrect ones are marked doubtful, go on to the next chapter. If not, review this chapter before taking the posttest.

of dialectal exceptions contains a half dozen miscellaneous words: *either, inveigle, leisure, neither, obeisance,* and *Pleiades.*

Review the more common of these exceptions now, before reading further, to fix them firmly in your mind.

THE "DEITY" WORDS—WITH TWO SEPARATE SOUNDS

> When the two letters are pronounced in different syllables, as in deity, the e comes before the i only if the first of the two sounds is an e.

The *e* sound comes first in *being, deify, reimburse, reinforce,* and *theistic;* therefore the *e* letter comes first, too. But the *e* sound does not come first in *anxiety, biennial, client, gaiety, society,* and *variety;* therefore the *e* letter does not come first in these words.

In most dialects in the United States this rule has no known exceptions. In a few American dialects, however, there are two small groups of exceptions. The first group is composed of such "Spanish" words as *fiesta, hacienda, San Diego,* and *siesta.* These "Spanish" words are exceptions in the dialects where the *i* is pronounced like an *e,* but not in other dialects.

The second group of exceptions includes words that have a final *y* in their simplest form, but change that *y* to an *ie* before a suffix is added. Examples of this group are *twentieth* (for *twenty*), *easier* (for *easy*), and *flashiest* (for *flashy*). In the dialects where this *i* is pronounced as an *e,* these words are exceptions; but they are not exceptions in any other dialects.

Notice also that *ei* occurs in compound words where the first word ends in a final silent *e* and the second begins with an *i,* as in *herein, therein,* and *wherein.* And notice, finally, the words *hoeing, shoeing, singeing,* and *tingeing,* which also have a final silent *e* before *ing.*

SUMMARY

In brief, use *i* before *e* unless the two letters are pronounced as in:

> The eight counterfeit steins deceived the deity.

That is the basic rule, on which all others depend. The exceptions, though fairly numerous, need not be overwhelming. The next grotesque sentence represents each kind:

> Sheila seized the fierce sheik's caffeine at the flashiest fiesta.

A few other words resist the rules and must, perhaps, be memorized. *Financier* resists by having *ie* after *c. Friend* and *mischief* resist, at least in some dialects, by having *ie* for the sound of short *i* (as in *bit*) in nonfinal positions. *Heifer* has *ei* for the sound of short *e* (as in *bet*), and *reveille* has *ei* for the "uh" sound discussed in Chapter 5—two sounds for which no spelling has been specified in this chapter.

If all these rules and exceptions (which are necessary for accuracy) seem too complicated for quick and ready use, then you may try another method for dealing with the *ie-ei* spellings—a keen sense of doubt. Already, merely by reading this chapter, you have begun to develop that sense of doubt. In the future continue to develop it by being exceedingly suspicious of *ie-ei* spellings, as suspicious of them as you are of square apples. Then, if your dictionary is nearby, your sense of doubt may guide you safely through the pitfalls of *ie-ei* spellings.

EXERCISE 10

Put *ie* or *ei* in each blank. If you are doubtful about your choice, mark the "D" column.

	D			D
1. ach __ vement	___	**11.** fr __ ght	___
2. rev __ lle	___	**12.** prot __ ns	___
3. fr __ nd	___	**13.** sl __ ght of hand	___
4. p __ rce	___	**14.** d __ ty	___
5. surf __ t	___	**15.** l __ utenant	___
6. s __ zed	___	**16.** anc __ nt	___
7. for __ gn	___	**17.** dy __ ng	___
8. v __ w	___	**18.** effic __ ntly	___
9. dec __ ve	___	**19.** l __ sure	___
10. counterf __ t	___	**20.** st __ n	___

For answers see box on page 91.

ANSWERS, POSTTEST 9

1. proceeded
2. statue
3. criticize
4. quite
5. concede
6. conscious
7. choose
8. succeed
9. personnel
10. whether

POSTTEST 10

Put *ie* or *ei* in each blank. If you are doubtful about your choice, mark the "D" column.

	D		D
1. O'N __ ll	___	6. heav __ st	___
2. unw __ ldy	___	7. sc __ ntific	___
3. soc __ ty	___	8. spontan __ ty	___
4. San D __ go	___	9. med __ val	___
5. r __ nforcements	___	10. w __ rd	___

For answers see box on page 93.

PART III WORD-BUILDING AS A GUIDE

Words are constructed not only by combining individual letters but also by fitting larger word-parts together. These word-parts are prefabricated groups of letters which have a meaning of their own, and each part is used repeatedly in forming words, just as each letter is used repeatedly in forming words. Thus a comparatively small number of parts (and letters) can form a large number of words—in theory an infinity of words. That is why learning to spell a few word-parts can aid you in the spelling of many words.

How letters, word-parts, and whole words are related to each other is illustrated by this diagram:

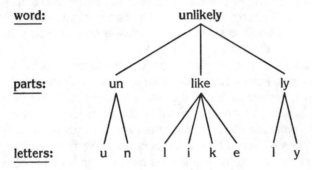

Here eight letters combine to form three parts, and then the three parts, in turn, combine to form a single whole word. Most words with two or more syllables are built in this way, by combining prefabricated groups of letters to form whole words.

These prefabricated word-parts are of three kinds: prefixes, suffixes, and stems. All three occur in the word **unlikely**. Here **un** is a prefix, which is added only at the beginning of a word; **ly** is a suffix, which is added only at the end; and **like** is a stem, the core to which the prefixes and suffixes may be added. They may be added in widely varying numbers and combinations, as, for example, in **un-like, like-ly, un-en-count-er-ed,** and **in-art-ist-ic-al-ly.**

For additional practice in constructing words by combining prefixes, stems, and suffixes, notice how these words have been formed: **tri-angle, non-sense, bi-foc-al, mis-in-form-ed, pre-mature-ly, ab-norm-al, de-code, fore-word, ex-pand-ing, un-know-able, for-bid, con-struct-ing,** and **anti-dis-estab-lish-ment-ar-ian-ism.**

When you become aware of the word-parts, you may begin to view the spelling of words not as an illogical combining of individual letters but rather as a logical combining of prefabricated prefixes, stems, and suffixes. You then think of the word **unlikely** not as a combination of eight letters but rather as a combination of a prefix, a stem, and a suffix—a combination of **un, like,** and **ly.**

Of course it is much easier to think of the three parts of that word than to think of its eight letters, simply because three is a smaller number than eight. Also it is much easier to think of the letters forming each part (two in **un,** four in **like,** and two in **ly**) than to think of all the eight letters in the whole word. The separate parts are easier to spell than whole words are, not only because they contain fewer letters, but also because you have had much more practice in spelling the parts than the whole. You have written **un** and **like** and **ly** much more often than you have written **unlikely.** Words which you write for the first time are often composed of parts which you have previously written (and therefore spelled) many times—they are just a new combination of old parts. For such reasons as these, knowledge of word-parts can be exceedingly helpful in spelling.

Another reason why knowledge of word-parts may be helpful is this: many trouble spots in spelling are located precisely where such word-parts are joined. At those very points the letters sometimes seem to behave in strange ways. Sometimes they are hyphenated **(co-owner)** and sometimes not **(coequal);** sometimes doubled **(conferred)** and sometimes not **(conference);** sometimes omitted (compare **change** with **changing**) and sometimes not (compare **change** with **changeable**); sometimes added (compare **tomato** with **tomatoes**) and sometimes not (compare **silo** with **silos**). Those troublesome problems, considered one by one in later chapters, can best be solved with the help of the principles of word-building, explained here.

For additional practice in word-building by combining word-parts, see the lists of frequently used prefixes and suffixes in Appendix E, page 173. Right now, while you are thinking about word-building, would be a good time for you to look at them. Later you may also want to refer to them again—that is why they are in an appendix: for quick reference.

ANSWERS, EXERCISE 10

1. achievement	11. freight
2. reveille	12. proteins
3. friend	13. sleight
4. pierce	14. deity
5. surfeit	15. lieutenant
6. seized	16. ancient
7. foreign	17. dyeing
8. view	18. efficiently
9. deceive	19. leisure
10. counterfeit	20. stein

If you got all the answers right or marked the wrong ones as doubtful, go on to the next chapter. If not, review this chapter before taking the posttest.

11

FINAL DOUBLING

PRETEST 11

Combine the stems and suffixes listed below, putting the proper spelling in the column labeled "Combined Form." If you are doubtful about your spelling, mark the "D" column.

Stem*	Suffix	Combined Form	D
1. commit	ed	_____	___
2. regret	ed	_____	___
3. control	able	_____	___
4. bed	side	_____	___
5. compel	ing	_____	___
6. scalp	ed	_____	___
7. occur	ence	_____	___
8. rid	ance	_____	___
9. thin	er	_____	___
10. forgot	en	_____	___

For answers see box on page 95.

THE PROBLEM

Why does *conferred* have two *r*'s, but *conference* only one? Likewise why does *preferred* have two, but *preference* only one? And why does *referred* have two, but *reference* only one?

---

*Some words in this column contain more than the stem.

THE FIRST CLUES

To discover the answer to those question, you are invited to become a detective for a few minutes, examining some clues or evidence and then, by reasoning, reaching a conclusion. Here is the first cluster of clues, which you should study before reading on:

With Doubling	Without Doubling
equipped	equipment
fattest	fatness
fitter	fitful
shipping	shipment

Analyze those words, breaking them down into their parts, and you discover that they consist of four stems (*equip, fat, fit,* and *ship*), with suffixes added to them (*ed, est, er, ing, ment, ness,* and *ful*). A closer examination shows that what is doubled in the first column (but not in the second) is the last letter of the stem—a consonant. (That is why this chapter could have been called "Doubling Final Consonants.") Now you are ready for the crucial question: how (except for the doubling) do the words in the first column differ from those in the second? That difference presumably explains why there is doubling in one column, but not in the other. Write down that difference here and now—before you reach the point in this chapter where that difference is stated:

_____

_____

ANSWERS, POSTTEST 10

1. O'Neill
2. unwieldy
3. society
4. San Diego
5. reinforcements

6. heaviest
7. scientific
8. spontaneity
9. medieval
10. weird

THE SECOND CLUES

Here is the second bit of evidence for you to consider:

With Doubling	Without Doubling
blotting	blocking
getting	itching
hitting	helping
skidding	scratching

Again each word consists of a stem with a suffix added to it. Again the last letter of the stem is doubled in one column, but not in the other. And again there is only one difference (besides the doubling) in all the words in one column and all in the other. When you spot that difference, write it down here, before you are later told what it is:

_____

_____

THE THIRD CLUES

The third set of clues:

With Doubling	Without Doubling
betting	beating
bedding	bleeding
beginning	gaining
rotting	routing

How (except for the doubling) do all the words in the first column differ from all in the second? Write your answer here:

_____

_____

THE FINAL CLUES

The last evidence to be considered:

With Doubling	Without Doubling
conferred	conference
deferred	deference
preferred	preference
referred	reference

This evidence may be the most mystifying that you have encountered because the key difference in the words in the two columns (besides the doubling) is not to be found in the spellings. Rather, it is to be found in the pronunciations. So pronounce the pairs of words aloud until you discover that difference, and then state that difference here:

_____

_____

THE CONCLUSION

Earlier word-sleuths have reached these conclusions about the evidence that you have examined: the final consonants of stem are doubled (1) when the added suffix begins with a vowel, as in *equipped,* but not when it begins with a consonant, as in *equipment;* (2) when the final consonant is a single one, as in *blot* and *get,* but not when it is a member

---

ANSWERS, PRETEST 11

1. committed
2. regretted
3. controllable
4. bedside
5. compelling
6. scalped
7. occurrence
8. riddance
9. thinner
10. forgotten

If you got all answers right or marked all your wrong ones as doubtful, go on to the next chapter. If not, study this chapter first.

of a cluster of consonants, as in *block* and *itch;* (3) when only a single vowel comes before the final consonant, as in *bet* and *bed,* but not when two vowels come before it, as in *beating* and *bleeding;* and (4) when the syllable with the final consonant is heavily stressed (or pronounced with special emphasis), as in *conferred,* but not when some other syllable is most heavily stressed, as in *conference.*

All that evidence has been distilled into a rule:

> *If a single final consonant in a stem has a single vowel before it and is in a stressed syllable, double it before a suffix beginning with a vowel.*

Of course that rule is fully illustrated by *conferred,* whose stem *(confer)* has a single final consonant *(r)* with a single vowel *(e)* before it in a stressed syllable *(conFERRed),* and the added suffix *(ed)* begins with a vowel *(e).*

The rule for doubling final consonants may seem forbiddingly complicated (Did you notice the double *d* in *forbiddingly?*), but there is a short cut that you can use as an aid for spelling. Simply use the word *conferred* as a model for doubling the final consonant. If a word is like *conferred,* double the consonant; if not, do not. That word can easily serve as a yardstick for measuring other words for doubling—a touchstone for quickly resolving the complicated problem. Here is a picture of that touchstone:

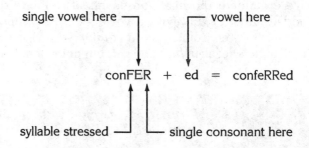

Of course, another shortcut is your sense of doubt, which may have been increased considerably by your work with this chapter, as you explored the intricacies of doubled final consonants in English. If this chapter has made you more suspicious about doubled final consonants, even if it has not made you a master of them, it has accomplished one of its purposes.

What is really recommended, though, is that you use *conferred* as a touchstone. Try it as you do the next exercise.

EXERCISE 11

Combine the stems and suffixes listed below, putting the proper spelling in the column labeled "Combined Form." If you are doubtful about your spelling, mark the "D" column.

Stem*	Suffix	Combined Form	D
1. commit	ment	_____	—
2. flood	ing	_____	—
3. begin	er	_____	—
4. refer	al	_____	—
5. travel	er	_____	—
6. prefer	ence	_____	—
7. shock	ing	_____	—
8. quiz	es	_____	—
9. transmit	ing	_____	—
10. win	ing	_____	—
11. transfer	ed	_____	—
12. drink	er	_____	—
13. plan	ed	_____	—
14. gag	ing	_____	—
15. repel	ent	_____	—
16. condemn	ing	_____	—
17. bag	age	_____	—
18. rip	ing	_____	—
19. reap	ed	_____	—
20. concur	ed	_____	—

For answers see box on page 99.

*Some words in this column contain more than the stem.

POSTTEST 11

Combine the stems and suffixes listed below, putting the proper spelling in the column labeled "Combined Form." If you are doubtful about your spelling, mark the "D" column.

Stem*	Suffix	Combined Form	D
1. god	ess	_____	____
2. marvel	ous	_____	____
3. regret	ful	_____	____
4. propel	ant	_____	____
5. worship	ed	_____	____
6. hop	ing	_____	____
7. confer	ence	_____	____
8. rebel	ious	_____	____
9. spin	er	_____	____
10. submit	ing	_____	____

For answers see box on page 101.

---

*Some words in this column contain more than the stem.

12

FINAL E

PRETEST 12

Combine the following stems and suffixes in the blank for the "Combined Form." If you are doubtful about your spelling of the combined form, mark the "D" column.

Stem*	Suffix	Combined Form	D
1. lose	ing	_____	___
2. bereave	ment	_____	___
3. here	in	_____	___
4. live	able	_____	___

*Some words in this column contain more than the stem.

ANSWERS, EXERCISE 11

1. commitment	11. transferred
2. flooding	12. drinker
3. beginner	13. planned
4. referral	14. gagging
5. traveler	15. repellent
6. preference	16. condemning
7. shocking	17. baggage
8. quizzes	18. ripping
9. transmitting	19. reaped
10. winning	20. concurred

If you got all answers right or marked the wrong ones as doubtful, go on to the next chapter. If not, review this chapter before taking the posttest.

5. safe   ty   _____   ____

6. conceive   able   _____   ____

7. shape   ing   _____   ____

8. argue   ment   _____   ____

9. behave   ing   _____   ____

10. improve   ment   _____   ____

For answers see box on page 103.

THE PROBLEM

Why does the final _e_ of _move_ drop out in _moving_ but remain in _movement_? Likewise, why does it drop out in _living_ (from _live_) but remain in _lively_? The answers are to be found in a rule.

THE RULE

The rule is quite simple:

**Final silent e is dropped before a suffix beginning with a vowel.**

Notice that the _e_ must be silent, as in _hope_ and _advise_. If it is pronounced, it stays before the added suffix. Contrast _hoping_ with _being_ and _advising_ with _fleeing_.

Notice also that the final _e_ must be the only vowel at the end of the word. In such words as _canoe, hoe, shoe,_ and _toe,_ the _e_ does not disappear before a suffix beginning with a vowel: _canoeing, hoeing, shoeing,_ and _toeing._ For the same reason it does not disappear after _y_ when _y_ is pronounced as a vowel: _dye_ becomes _dyeing_, with the _e_ kept.

In addition, notice that the suffix must begin with a vowel if the _e_ is to disappear. For instance, contrast the behavior of the _e_ in these words: _caring_ and _careful, hoping_ and _hopeless, movable_ and _movement,_ and _usable_ and _useful._

Notice, finally, that _e_ disappears only before a suffix, not before a whole word added to form a compound word. Thus the _e_ of _pine_ disappears in _pining_, but stays in _pineapple;_ the _e_ disappears in _giving_, but stays in _giveaway._ And, of course, it stays in such compound words as _thereafter, therein, whereabouts,_ and _whereupon._

In brief, final silent _e_ is dropped before a suffix beginning with a vowel, but is kept in all other situations. This simple rule applies to thousands of words—perhaps to more than are covered by any other spelling rule. So knowing this rule is especially important.

What happens to final silent *e* is controlled not only by that rule but also by a subrule that applies only to words with a *c* or *g* just before the final *e*.

THE C-G SUBRULE

Here is the subrule stated in its simplest form:

> When right after *c* or *g*, the final silent *e* is kept before the suffixes *able* and *ous*.

For instance, the *e* is kept in *noticeable,* but dropped in *noticing,* which does not have either of the suffixes required for retention. Likewise, the *e* is kept in *courageous,* but dropped in *encouraging,* which does not have either of the suffixes required for retention.

The operation of the *c-g* subrule is also illustrated by a comparison of *changeable* with *changing, gorgeous* with *gorging, manageable* with *managing, outrageous* with *raging, replaceable* with *replacing, serviceable* with *servicing,* and *traceable* with *tracing.*

Perhaps the easiest way to master the *c-g* subrule is to associate it with the spelling of two words, *noticeable* and *courageous.* Those two illustrate the special letters involved, *c* and *g;* and they illustrate the special suffixes involved, *able* and *ous.* Thus *noticeable* and *courageous* can serve as models for the operation of the subrule, as touchstones for dealing with the *c-g* words.

Only two common words are exceptions to the subrule: *practicable* and *sacrilegious.* Of course *practicable* is a word that should, according to the subrule, retain the *e;* but it does not. Notice that the *c* in this

ANSWERS, POSTTEST 11

1. goddess	6. hopping
2. marvelous	7. conference
3. regretful	8. rebellious
4. propellant	9. spinner
5. worshiped	10. submitting

exceptional word is pronounced like a *k*, while the *c* in the words conforming to the rule is pronounced like an *s*. At one time scribes signaled the *s* pronunciation of *c* by keeping the *e* (as in *noticeable*) and signaled the *k* pronunciation by dropping the *e* (as in *practicable*). They also used the retained *e* to signal the *j* pronunciation of *g* (contrast the pronunciation of *g* in *gem* and *get*)—an additional reason for the *c-g* subrule.

Sacrilegious (from *sacrilege*) is often misspelled for two reasons. First, it has an *i*, not an *e*, right after the *g*—that is why it is an exception. Second, its middle syllables are spelled *rileg* instead of *relig*, as they would be in *religion*. Because the meaning of *sacrilegious* is associated with that of *religion*, the temptation is strong to spell that part of the word like a part of *religion*—really to misspell it that way. For those two reasons *sacrilegious* is one of the most difficult words in the language to spell right. But a sacrilegious person is NOT a religious person—a reason why *religious* should NOT be a part of *sacrilegious*.

Now you see why four words can guide you in using the *c-g* subrule: *noticeable, courageous, practicable*, and *sacrilegious*.

EXCEPTIONS TO THE MAIN RULE

Just as there are a few exceptions to the subrule, so are there a few to the main rule—a comparatively small number in comparison with the multitudes of words covered by the main rule.

Most exceptions violate the rule in a single way: by dropping the *e* even before suffixes beginning with consonants. That *e* is dropped (at least in the United States*) for many words with *dge* before the suffix *ment* is added: *abridgment, acknowledgment, judgment*, and *lodgment*. It is dropped in words ending *ue*, as in *argument, duly*, and *truly*. It is dropped before the suffix *th*, as in *ninth, twelfth*, and *width*. If a word ends in *le*, that *e* is dropped, along with the *l* itself, when an *ly* suffix is added: *doubly, incredibly, possibly, probably, subtly*, and *wholly*. And it is dropped in three other miscellaneous words: *awful, nursling*, and *wisdom*.

Only three common words violate the rule in the other way: by keeping the final *e* before a suffix beginning with a vowel. All three involve the same suffix, *age: acreage, lineage*, and *mileage*.

Almost all the exceptions cited in the last two paragraphs are words which you are likely to use at almost any time, and most of them occur in lists of words often misspelled. That is why a review of those excep-

---

*For an explanation of this difference between American and British spelling, see pages 134-136.

tions, right now, may be justified. Some of them are included in the following exercise.

EXERCISE 12

Combine the stems and suffixes in the blank for the "Combined Form." If you are doubtful about the spelling of the combined form, mark the "D" column.

Stem*	Suffix	Combined Form	D
1. advantage	ous	_____	___
2. value	able	_____	___
3. complete	ing	_____	___
4. amuse	ment	_____	___
5. notice	able	_____	___
6. lodge	ment	_____	___
7. love	ly	_____	___
8. nine	ty	_____	___
9. care	ing	_____	___
10. achieve	ment	_____	___
11. charge	able	_____	___
12. practice	al	_____	___
13. courage	ous	_____	___

*Some words in this column contain more than the stem.

ANSWERS, PRETEST 12

1. losing	6. conceivable
2. bereavement	7. shaping
3. herein	8. argument
4. livable	9. behaving
5. safety	10. improvement

14. marriage   able   _____   ____
15. commute   ing   _____   ____
16. due   ly   _____   ____
17. where   in   _____   ____
18. strive   ing   _____   ____
19. wise   dom   _____   ____
20. hate   ful   _____   ____

For answers see box on page 107.

POSTTEST 12

Combine the stems and suffixes in the blank for "Combined Form." If you are doubtful of your spelling, mark the "D" column.

Stem*	Suffix	Combined Form	D
1. mile	age	_____	____
2. true	ly	_____	____
3. excuse	able	_____	____
4. commence	ment	_____	____
5. nerve	ous	_____	____
6. cripple	ing	_____	____
7. dole	ful	_____	____
8. sense	ible	_____	____
9. judge	ment	_____	____
10. assemble	age	_____	____

For answers see box on page 109.

---

*Some words in this column contain more than the stem.

13

ASSIMILATIVE
DOUBLING

PRETEST 13

If a letter is needed in the blank, insert it. If you are doubtful about the spelling, mark the "D" column.

		D				D
1.	co __ nect	___	**6.**	i __ mediate	___
2.	su __ press	___	**7.**	co __ lege	___
3.	o __ mitted	___	**8.**	a __ paratus	___
4.	i __ measurable	___	**9.**	i __ rational	___
5.	o __ riginal	___	**10.**	a __ gression	___

For answers see box on page 111.

THE CAUSE OF THE DOUBLING

Long ago the prefix *sub*, meaning "under," and the stem *port*, meaning "to carry," were joined to form the word *subport*, meaning "to carry from underneath." At that time both the *b* and *p* were pronounced and were also included in the spelling. Since then two changes have occurred in the pronunciation of the word while only one has occurred in its spelling. First the *b* sound changed into a *p* sound, and the spelling therefore became *support*, with a double *p*. Then the *p* sound began to be pronounced just once, instead of twice, but the spelling did not change. Thus the second *p*, gone from the pronunciation, persists in the spelling as a vestige of an earlier pronunciation, just as the vermiform appendix persists in man as a vestige of an earlier stage of his evolution.

Why did the *b* sound of *sub* change into a *p* sound? That change was caused by a phonetic process called "assimilation," a process which operates in all languages that have so far been examined by scholars.

What happens is that similar sounds, when thrown next to each other, become identical. The *b* and *p* sounds are similar, pronounced just alike except for one thing: your vocal cords, near your Adam's apple, are vibrating when you pronounce *b*, but are not vibrating when you pronounce *p*. If you put two fingers against your Adam's apple and pronounce the two sounds—first *b-b-b* and then *p-p-p*—you will feel with your fingertips those vibrations with *b*, but not with *p*. When those two sounds were thrown together in *subport*, long ago, speakers had to do something complicated. For the *b*, they had to close and open their lips while they vibrated their vocal cords and then, in a split second, they had to close and open their lips again for the *p*, this time without vibrating their vocal cords.

So speakers began to simplify the pronunciation of the word. First they stopped vibrating their vocal cords for the *b* sound, which then automatically became a *p* sound. It was at that stage that the spelling of *support* with two *p*'s began. Next the speakers stopped closing and opening their lips twice in a split second for the two *p* sounds—once, they thought, was enough. The result was that the *pp* began to be pronounced *p*, as it is today. But the spelling with *pp* has, like the vermiform appendix, persisted down to the present.*

What has happened to *support* has also happened to hundreds of other words. As a result, hundreds of words are spelled with doubled letters which are pronounced as a single letter. Because spelling so often tends to follow pronunciation, these hundreds of words are frequently misspelled in the same way; they have a letter once *(suport)* where they should have it twice *(support)*.

Assimilation caused doubling only where the last sound of the prefix happened to be similar to the first sound of the stem. That is why the *sub* prefix survives, unchanged, in many words like *subconscious, subdue, subjugate, submarine,* and *subordinate*. But when the last sound of *sub* happened to be similar to the first sound of the stem, doubling occurred. That explains the doubled *f* in *suffer* ("to bear under"), *suffix* ("to attach under"), and *suffuse* ("to fuse beneath"). Also assimilation explains the doubled *p* in *supplant, supplicate, support,* and *suppress;* and the double *r* in *surrender, surreptitious,* and *surround*. Notice that the doubled letter always represents not the last sound of the prefix but the first sound of the stem.

What has happened to the prefix *sub* may be illustrated by this diagram:

---

*For another example of how assimilation has led to a change in pronunciation and then to a frequent misspelling, see the discussion of *used to,* pages 50-56. For more on the contrast between voiced and unvoiced sounds, see page 74.

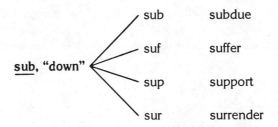

Just as assimilation led to doubling when *sub* was attached to certain stems, so has assimilation led to doubling when other prefixes have been attached to certain stems. Among these other suffixes are *ad, com, in,* and *ob,* which will now be considered one by one.

AD

Ad, meaning "to," remains unchanged in *adhere* ("to stick to"). But it became *ac* before a *c,* as in *accent, accept, access, accident, accommodate, accompany, accumulate,* and *accustomed.* It became *af* in *affiliate, affix, afflict,* and *afford.* It became *ag* in *agglomerate, aggravate, aggregation,* and *aggression.* It became *al* in *allege, allegiance, alliance, allot, allow, allude,* and *allure.* And it became *an* in *announce* and *an-*

ANSWERS, EXERCISE 12

1. advantageous	11. chargeable
2. valuable	12. practical
3. completing	13. courageous
4. amusement	14. marriageable
5. noticeable	15. commuting
6. lodgment	16. duly
7. lovely	17. wherein
8. ninety	18. striving
9. caring	19. wisdom
10. achievement	20. hateful

If you got all answers right or marked the wrong ones doubtful, go on to the next chapter. If not, review this chapter before taking the posttest.

nex; ap in *appear* and *appoint; as* in *assert* and *assign;* and so on. Like a chameleon adjusting to the colors nearest it, *ad* has adjusted to many of the sounds nearest it. This diagram illustrates its varied forms:

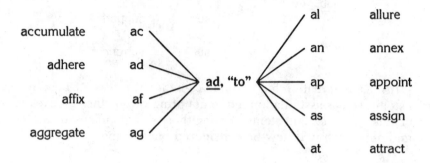

COM

The Latin word *cum,* meaning "with," has become a prefix in English, spelled *com* except where it has been assimilated into some other form. In *compassion* ("with feeling"), *compel* ("with force"), and numerous other words it retains its customary form. But before stems beginning with certain other sounds it is converted into a different form. It becomes *col* in *collect* ("to gather with") and *collide* ("to strike with"). It becomes *con* in *connect* ("to bind with") and *connive* ("to wink with"). And it becomes *cor* in *correlate* ("to relate with") and *correspond* ("to respond with"). The diagram summarizes the story:

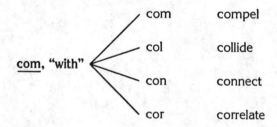

IN

Perhaps the prefix which has produced the largest number of assimilative doublings is *in,* meaning "not," as in *incapable* and *insane.* It caused the double *l* in *illegal, illegible, illiterate,* and *illogical;* the double *m* in *immature, immediate* (literally "without a middle"), *immense, immobilized, immoderate, immodest,* and *immoral;* and the double *r* in *irrational, irregular, irrelevant, irresponsible,* and *irreverent.* Here is a summarizing diagram for the assimilated forms of *in,* with the "not" meaning:

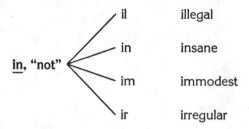

Two prefixes, with two different meanings, are spelled *in* in English. In addition to the one meaning "not," there is also one meaning "in," and it, too, participates in assimilative doubling. It is not assimilated in the word *inhabit,* but is assimilated in such words as *illuminate, immigrate,* and *irradiate.* As the next diagram shows, the assimilated forms of this prefix are the same as those for the other *in* prefix—*il, im,* and *ir:*

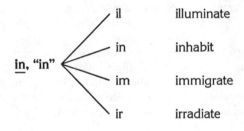

ANSWERS, POSTTEST 12

1. mileage	6. crippling
2. truly	7. doleful
3. excusable	8. sensible
4. commencement	9. judgment
5. nervous	10. assemblage

OB

Still another chameleon-like prefix is *ob*, meaning "against," as in *ob-stacle*, meaning "something which stands against something else." Its assimilation has caused the doublings in *occasion* and *occupation*, in *offend* and *offer*, and in *oppose* and *oppress*.

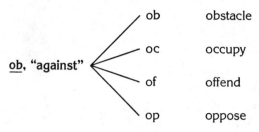

SUMMARY

Here are the most important prefixes that participate in assimilative doubling:

Prefix	Meaning	Sample Words
ad	to	adhere, accumulate, affix, aggregation, allure, appoint, assign
com	with	compare, collaborate, connect, correspond
in[1]	not	insane, illegal, immodest, irrational
in[2]	in	illuminate, inhabit, immigrate, irradiate
ob	against	obstacle, occupation, offend, oppose
sub	under	submarine, suffuse, suppress, surreptitious.

In all those words at least the first letter of the prefix has persisted, and in almost all, the meaning, too, has persisted. These two clues—the first letter and the meaning—can guide you in getting your assimilative doublings right.

APPARENT EXCEPTIONS

A few common words look as though they have assimilated prefixes, but, in fact, they do not. They begin with the same letters as the assimilative prefixes. But they do not express the meanings of those prefixes, and, as a result, they do not have assimilative doubling. For example, the *im* of *image* and *imagination* is different from the *im* of *immature* and *immigrate*. The *im* of *image* does not mean "not" or "in." So *image* and *imagination* do not have assimilative doubling.

Likewise, no assimilative doubling has occurred in *omit, omission, orange, origin,* and *original,* for these words obviously were not constructed with the prefix *ob,* meaning "against." Also, *surprise* does not contain a double *p,* as *suppress* does, because *surprise* was not constructed with the prefix *sub,* "under."

You see, the first letter or two AND the meaning of the prefix will guide you accurately in dealing with assimilative doubling; both clues must be considered. For further practice in dealing with this sort of doubling, do the next exercise.

EXERCISE 13

If a letter is needed in the blank, insert it. If you are doubtful about a spelling, mark the "D" column.

	D		D
1. a __ semble	_____	11. i __ regular	____
2. su __ port	_____	12. su __ position	____
3. o __ position	_____	13. a __ sumption	____
4. co __ league	_____	14. di __ similar	____
5. a __ nexation	_____	15. a __ tract	____
6. i __ legible	_____	16. o __ range	____
7. re __ semble	_____	17. o __ cupy	____
8. di __ ferent	_____	18. i __ migrate	____
9. a __ pear	_____	19. i __ luminate	____
10. co __ lection	_____	20. a __ range	____

For answers see box on page 113.

For answers see box on page 113.

ANSWERS, PRETEST 13

1. connect
2. suppress
3. omitted
4. immeasurable
5. original
6. immediate
7. college
8. apparatus
9. irrational
10. aggression

If you got all answers right or marked all wrong ones as doubtful, go on to the next chapter. If not, study this chapter first.

POSTTEST 13

If a letter is needed in the blank, insert it. If you are doubtful about a spelling, mark the "D" column.

	D		D
1. o __ cur	___	6. i __ magination	___
2. co __ mittee	___	7. o __ fensive	___
3. a __ signment	___	8. a __ pointed	___
4. a. __ ligned	___	9. su __ prise	___
5. co __ lapsed	___	10. i __ literate	___

For answers see box on page 115.

14

ADDITIVE
DOUBLING

PRETEST 14

Combine the following word-parts in the blanks provided. If you are doubtful about your spellings, mark the "D" column.

Prefix	Stem*	Suffix	Combined Form	D
1. over	run		_____	___
2. re	enact	ment	_____	___
3. with	hold	ing	_____	___

*Some words in this column contain more than the stem.

ANSWERS, EXERCISE 13

1. assemble
2. support
3. opposition
4. colleague
5. annexation
6. illegible
7. resemble
8. different
9. appear
10. collection

11. irregular
12. supposition
13. assumption
14. dissimilar
15. attract
16. orange
17. occupy
18. immigrate
19. illuminate
20. arrange

If you got all answers right or marked the wrong ones as doubtful, go on to the next chapter. If not, review this chapter before taking the posttest.

4. un	civil	ly	_____	___
5. in	numer	able	_____	___
6. co	ordinate		_____	___
7.	sudden	ness	_____	___
8. un	help	ful, ly	_____	___
9. inter	relation	ship	_____	___
10. un	need	ed	_____	___

For answers see box on page 117.

When two words or word-parts are combined to form a bigger word, doubling occurs if the letters thus brought together are the same. For instance, if *with* is combined with *hold*, the result is *withhold*, with the *h* doubled. Likewise, if the prefix *un* is combined with the stem *necessary*, the result is *unnecessary*, with the *n* doubled. And if the stem *cool* is combined with the suffix *ly*, the result is *coolly*, with the *l* doubled. Those additive doublings stand out even more clearly when capitalized: *witHHold, uNNecessary*, and *cooLLy*.

Additive doubling sometimes occurs twice in the same word, once with the adding of a prefix to the word and the second time with the adding of a suffix to the same word. Such a doubling is illustrated by *unnaturally*. There the doubled *n* was caused by combining the prefix *un* with the word *natural*, while the doubled *l* was caused by combining the suffix *ly* with the same word. Again the additive doublings stand out more clearly when capitalized: *uNNaturaLLy*.

The reason why additive doublings cause trouble in spelling is that they are, at one time or another, pronounced in three different ways. Sometimes both letters are pronounced, as in *unneeded*. At other times only one of them is pronounced, as in *really*. And in at least one word neither is pronounced: *knickknack*. (The silent double *k* in that word is one of the freaks of English spelling.)

Because spelling tends to follow pronunciation, words like *unneeded*, where both letters are pronounced, cause little trouble in spelling. Preposterous spellings like *knickknack*, simply because they are so preposterous, also cause little trouble. The worst troublemakers are words like *really* and *coolly*, where there are two letters in the spelling, but only one sound in the pronunciation. Those are the tricky additive doublings, the treacherous ones, which should be treated with suspicion and doubt. Here again is the rule for additive doubling:

When two words or word-parts are combined to form a bigger word, doubling occurs if the letters thus brought together are the same.

And the opposite is also true: if the combining does not bring the same letters together, then doubling does not occur. Contrast *dissatisfy* with *disown, inte.relationship* with *interview, misspelling* with *mistake, overrated* with *overheated, unneeded* with *unleashed, soulless* with *soulful, really* with *reality,* and *meanness* with *meaning.*

EXERCISE 14

Combine the following word-parts in the blanks provided. If you are doubtful about your spelling, mark the "D" column.

Prefix	Stem*	Suffix	Combined Form	D
1. un	adapt	able	_____	___
2. re	appraise		_____	___
3. mis	shaped		_____	___
4. re	educate		_____	___
5. un	mistaken		_____	___
6. dis	sect	ing	_____	___
7. un	noticed		_____	___
8.	final	ly	_____	___
9. inter	racial		_____	___
10. co	operate		_____	___
11. in	complete	ly	_____	___
12. un	natural	ly	_____	___

*Some words in this column contain more than the stem.

13. over   ride   _____   ___

14. inter   ruption   _____   ___

15. un   necessary   _____   ___

16. over   rate   _____   ___

17.   thin   ness   _____   ___

18. dis   satisfy   _____   ___

19. mis   spell   ing   _____   ___

20.   art   ful, ly   _____   ___

For answers see box on page 119.

POSTTEST 14

Combine the following word-parts in the blanks provided. If you are doubtful about your spelling, mark the "D" column.

Prefix	Stem*	Suffix	Combined Form	D
1.	cruel	ly	_____	___
2. re	enlist	ed	_____	___
3. out	talk	ed	_____	___
4. mis	state	ment	_____	___
5. re	examine		_____	___
6. un	fear	ful, ly	_____	___
7. trans	ship	ment	_____	___
8. un	real	ly	_____	___
9. pre	establish	ment	_____	___
10.	drunken	ness	_____	___

For answers see box on page 121.

---

*Some words in this column contain more than the stem.

PRETEST 15

Combine the following stems and suffixes. Mark the "D" column if you are doubtful about your spelling.

Stem*	Suffix	Combined Form	D
1. bury	al	_____	___
2. turkey	s	_____	___
3. ugly	est	_____	___
4. multiply	ing	_____	___
5. attorney	s	_____	___
6. marry	ed	_____	___
7. carry	ing	_____	___
8. empty	ness	_____	___

*Some words in this column contain more than the stem.

ANSWERS, PRETEST 14

1. overrun
2. reenactment
3. withholding
4. uncivilly
5. innumerable
6. coordinate
7. suddenness
8. unhelpfully
9. interrelationship
10. unneeded

If all your answers were right or if you marked all wrong ones as doubtful, go on to the next chapter. If not, study this chapter first.

   9. alley   s   _____   ____

   10. accompany   ist   _____   ____

For answers see box on page 123.

Final *y* behaves in two different ways when suffixes are added to it. If it occurs after a vowel, as in *alley,* it remains unchanged before an added suffix, as in *alleys.* But if it occurs after a consonant, as in *ally,* it is changed to *i,* as in *allies.*

THE RULE

That behavior is described in a brief rule:

   If after a consonant, final y *becomes* i *before an added suffix.*

The change to *i* is illustrated by *apologies, duties,* and *mercies*—all of them with a consonant before the final *y.* And the retention of the *y* is illustrated by *attorneys, chimneys,* and *monkeys*—all of them with a vowel before the *y.* Further examples of the operation of this rule are the contrasts between *babied* and *buoyed, carrier* and *conveyer, emptiness* and *employable.* As these examples show, the crucial question is whether the final *y* is preceded by a consonant or a vowel.

   Two kinds of suffixes keep the *y* from changing to *i.* One is the possessive suffix, illustrated by *Mary's* and *somebody's* (not *Maries* and *somebodies*). The other is a suffix beginning with an *i* as in *marrying, copyist,* and *fortyish.* So the rule is more accurate in this expanded form: if after a consonant, final *y* becomes *i* before a suffix unless the suffix begins with *i* or shows possession.

THE EXCEPTIONS

The exceptions to this rule cause very little trouble. Most people know how to spell them automatically, without even considering whether they conform to or depart from any rule. As a result, the exceptions rarely occur on lists of words most frequently misspelled, and the chances are that you do not need to spend time in memorizing the exceptions. For practical purposes, all that you need to know about them is that they exist.

   Glance, though, at this list of some of the most common exceptions:

   1. Proper names keep the *y* (*Berrys* and *Sallys*), but common nouns replace it with *i* (*berries* and *sallies*).

2. Longer words often lose the *y* entirely before a suffix beginning with *i*, as in *accompanist* and *militarism*.

3. Some common short words change *y* to *i* even after a vowel, as in *daily, gaily, laid,* and *slain.*

Final *y* will probably cause you little or no trouble if you understand fully the spelling of only three key words: *allies* (after a consonant), *alleys* (after a vowel), and *studying* (before *i*)—and if you remember that there are some exceptions that you probaly know how to spell already.

EXERCISE 15

Combine the following stems and suffixes. Mark the "D" column if you are doubtful about your spelling.

Stem*	Suffix	Combined Form	D
1. verify	ed	_____	___
2. steady	ing	_____	___

*Some words in this column contain more than the stem.

ANSWERS, EXERCISE 14

1. unadaptable
2. reappraise
3. misshaped
4. reeducate
5. unmistaken
6. dissecting
7. unnoticed
8. finally
9. interracial
10. cooperate
11. incompletely
12. unnaturally
13. override
14. interruption
15. unnecessary
16. overrate
17. thinness
18. dissatisfy
19. misspelling
20. artfully

If you got all answers right or marked all wrong answers as doubtful, go on to the next chapter. If not, review this chapter before taking the posttest.

3. simplify	cation	_____	___
4. Barry	s	_____	___
5. worry	ed	_____	___
6. ski	ing	_____	___
7. funny	est	_____	___
8. money	ed	_____	___
9. clarify	cation	_____	___
10. terrify	ing	_____	___
11. honey	ed	_____	___
12. taxi	ing	_____	___
13. donkey	s	_____	___
14. magnify	ing	_____	___
15. alimony	es	_____	___
16. folly	es	_____	___
17. doily	es	_____	___
18. signify	ing	_____	___
19. allay	ed	_____	___
20. comply	ed	_____	

For answers see box on page 125.

POSTTEST 15

Combine the following stems and suffixes. Mark the "D" column if you are doubtful about your spelling.

Stem	Suffix	Combined Form	D
1. study	ed	_____	___
2. mercy	ful	_____	___
3. monkey	ed	_____	___
4. baby	ing	_____	___
5. military	ism	_____	___
6. ally	ed	_____	___

7. Berry	s	_____	____
8. gay	ly	_____	____
9. chimney	s	_____	____
10. berry	s	_____	____

For answers see box on page 127.

For answers see box on page 127.

ANSWERS, POSTTEST 14

1. cruelly	6. unfearfully
2. reenlisted	7. transshipment
3. outtalked	8. unreally
4. misstatement	9. preestablishment
5. reexamine	10. drunkenness

16

OTHER FINAL LETTERS

PRETEST 16

Combine the following stems and suffixes. Mark the "D" column where you are doubtful about your spelling.

Stem	Suffix	Combined Form	D
1. traffic	ing	_____	___
2. piano	s	_____	___
3. bush	s	_____	___
4. thief	s	_____	___
5. witch	s	_____	___
6. fizz	s	_____	___
7. roof	s	_____	___
8. echo	s	_____	___
9. mimic	ed	_____	___
10. moss	s	_____	___

For answers see box on page 129.

Certain other final letters besides *e* (Chapter 12) and *y* (Chapter 15) behave in special ways before a suffix is added. Among them are *c*, *o*, and *f*; a few letters with hissing sounds; and some possessive forms.

FINAL C

Normally *c* is pronounced as *s* before *e* and *i*, as in *center* and *civil*. So when it is pronounced as *k* before these letters, a *k* is added to the spelling to signal that pronunciation. Such a *k* appears in *frolicKed*, *mimicKing, panicKed, picnicKing,* and *trafficKed.* But the *k* is not added in *noticing* (where the *c* is pronounced as *s*), nor is the *k* added in *frolicsome* (where the suffix begins with some letter other than *e* or *i*).

FINAL O

Words with a vowel before a final *o* are easy to deal with because they form their plural in the regular way, simply by the addition of an *s*. Examples include *cameos, radios, rodeos, Romeos,* and *studios.*

But a consonant before the final *o* causes trouble, for plurals of such words are sometimes formed with *s* and sometimes with *es*. Examples with *s* include *altos, hypos, pianos, quartos, silos,* and *solos.* Examples with *es* include *cargoes, echoes, embargoes, mottoes, potatoes,* and *to-matoes.*

Perhaps the best thing to do is to use *s* with all words having a vowel before the final *o*, but to consult a dictionary for the spelling of the words with a consonant before the final *o*.

FINAL F

Contrast *half* with *halves, leaf* with *leaves, self* with *selves,* and *thief* with *thieves.* These examples show that words with final *f* normally are pluralized, not by *fs*, but by *ves*.

Your pronunciation can guide you in choosing between *fs* and *ves* in these words, for the exceptions to the rule for final *f* are spelled as

ANSWERS, PRETEST 15

1. burial	6. married
2. turkeys	7. carrying
3. ugliest	8. emptiness
4. multiplying	9. alleys
5. attorneys	10. accompanist

If you got all your answers right or marked all missed ones as doubt-ful, go on to the next chapter. If not, study this chapter before taking the posttest.

they are pronounced. Among these exceptions are *chiefs* (not *chieves*), *hoofs* (not *hooves*), and *roofs* (not *rooves*). Even when the dictionary gives two acceptable spellings—as for *scarfs-scarves* and for *wharfs-wharves*—you may spell the word as you pronounce it.

FINAL HISSING SOUNDS

Words with final hissing sounds also form their plurals with *es* instead of *s*, as in *churches, rushes, losses, Joneses, quizzes,* and *boxes*. Notice that the *es* in such words is always pronounced as a extra, an additional, syllable. Thus *search* has one syllable, but *searches*, two; *bush*, one, but *bushes*, two; *boss*, one, but *bosses*, two; *Williams*, two, but *Williamses*, three; *whiz*, one, but *whizzes*, two; and *tax*, one, but *taxes*, two. So the pronunciation of an extra syllable in such words may signal the need for a spelling with *es* rather than *s*.

POSSESSIVES WITH ES PLURALS

When plurals are formed by adding not just *s*, but *es*, possessives are formed by putting the apostrophe AFTER the *es*:

Singular	Singular Possessive	Plural Possessive
elf	elf's	elves'
church	church's	churches'
Jones	Jones's	Joneses'

EXERCISE 16

Combine the following stems and suffixes. Mark the "D" column where you are doubtful about your spelling.

Stem*	Suffix	Combined Form	D
1. picnic	ing	_____	___
2. shelf	ed	_____	___
3. motto	s	_____	___
4. twitch	s	_____	___
5. studio	s	_____	___

*Some words in this column contain more than the stem.

6. ax   s   _____   ___

7. gulch   s   _____   ___

8. Romeo   s   _____   ___

9. search   s   _____   ___

10. commando   s   _____   ___

11. boss   s   _____   ___

12. frolic   ed   _____   ___

13. soprano   s   _____   ___

14. chief   s   _____   ___

15. colic   y   _____   ___

16. switch   s   _____   ___

17. rodeo   s   _____   ___

18. mix   s   _____   ___

19. whiz   s   _____   ___

20. miss   s   _____   ___

For answers see box on page 131.

ANSWERS, EXERCISE 15

1. verified	11. honeyed
2. steadying	12. taxiing
3. simplification	13. donkeys
4. Barrys	14. magnifying
5. worried	15. alimonies
6. skiing	16. follies
7. funniest	17. doilies
8. moneyed	18. signifying
9. clarification	19. allayed
10. terrifying	20. complied

If you got all answers right or marked the wrong ones as doubtful, go on to the next chapter. If not, review this chapter before taking the posttest.

POSTTEST 16

Combine the following stems and suffixes. Mark the "D" column where you are doubtful about your spelling.

	Stem*	Suffix	Combined Form	D
1.	silo	s	_____	____
2.	relish	s	_____	____
3.	cameo	s	_____	____
4.	falsetto	s	_____	____
5.	Jones	's	_____	____
6.	panic	ing	_____	____
7.	cargo	s	_____	____
8.	leaf	s	_____	____
9.	belch	s	_____	____
10.	tomato	s	_____	____

For answers see box on page 133.

---

*Some words in this column contain more than the stem.

PART IV GUIDES FOR OTHER PROBLEMS

Three remaining problems in spelling are not caused primarily by pronunciation (Part II) or by word-building (Part III). These three remaining problems are considered in the next three chapters: "Internal Doubling," "Compound Words," and "Competing Spellings."

17

INTERNAL
DOUBLING

PRETEST 17

If needed, put a letter into the following blanks. If you are doubtful about your spelling, mark the "D" column.

		D				D
1.	tyra __ ny	___	**6.**	para __ lel	___
2.	fa __ lacy	___	**7.**	na __ rative	___
3.	bu __ letin	___	**8.**	inte __ ligent	___
4.	va __ cine	___	**9.**	vac __ um	___
5.	toba __ co	___	**10.**	exa __ gerate	___

For answers see box on page 135.

TROUBLESOME DOUBLING

Most doublings within the stems of words—illustrated by *feed, good, hall,* and *stuff*—cause no trouble at all and therefore are not dealt with here. But certain other internal doublings—illustrated by *accommodation, bulletin, embarrass,* and *vaccination*—are toublesome and deserve further attention. They are normally troublesome because only one of the doubled letters is pronounced, although both must be spelled.

There are three main methods for dealing with these words, methods that involve word-building, mnemonic devices, and memorizing.

WORD-BUILDING

The analysis of a word—that is, breaking it down into its prefixes, stem, and suffixes—frequently shows that what appeared to be internal doubling is really something else. It may be additive doubling (discussed in Chapter 14), assimilative doubling (Chapter 13), final doubling (Chapter 11), or even a combination of those doublings.

For example, in *accommodation* the double *c* is a result of assimilation (the prefix *ad*, "to," became *ac*), and the double *m* is the result of adding the prefix *com*, "with," to the Latin stem *modus*, which meant "fitting" or "suitable." In the strictest sense, therefore, the word *accommodation* has no internal doubling (that is, no doubling within the stem), even though the double *m* comes near the middle of the word.

In the same way some other words that at first glance seem to have internal doubling will be discovered, if analyzed into their various parts, to have some other sort of doubling: assimilative, additive, or final.

Two words which long ago underwent assimilative doubling are *differ* and *intelligent*. The word *differ* was built by adding the prefix *dis*, "away," to the stem *ferre*, "to carry," as though unlike things should be carried away from each other or separated during classification; then the *dis* prefix was changed to *dif* by the assimilative process explained in Chapter 13. *Intelligent* was built with the prefix *inter*, "between," and the stem *lig*, "choose," plus the suffix *ent*, which makes the word an adjective. This time assimilation changed *inter* into *intel*, thus producing a double *l* near the middle of the word.

Two words with additive doubling near their middle are *recommend* and *symmetry*. *Recommend* was formed with two prefixes (*re*, "again," and *com*, "with") plus the stem *mend*, with the earlier meaning of "to mandate" or "to decree." Of course the additive doubling occurred when the *com* prefix was added to the *mend* stem. In the same way the double *m* in *symmetry* was produced when the Greek prefix *sym*, "same," was added to the Greek stem *met*, "measure."

Also, the rule for doubling the final consonant before a suffix beginning with a vowel (Chapter 11) caused doubling inside at least three

ANSWERS, PRETEST 16

1. trafficking
2. pianos
3. bushes
4. thieves
5. witches
6. fizzes
7. roofs
8. echoes
9. mimicked
10. mosses

If you got all answers right or marked your wrong ones doubtful, go on to the next chapter. If not, study this chapter first.

words: *excellent, narrate,* and *necessary.* Thus *excel,* with one *l,* became *excellent,* with two, when the suffix *ent* was added. Before the suffix *ate,* the stem of *narrate,* which had one *r,* received a second *r.* Likewise the double *s* in *necessary* was caused by the vowel in its suffix, *ary.* Earlier the word meant "that which cannot be avoided," with the *ne* serving as the negative prefix, "not," and with the stem *ces* conveying "avoid."

The brief history of these eight words—*accommodate, differ, intelligent, recommend, symmetry, excellent, narrate,* and *necessary*—may help you to remember that a letter near their middle is doubled in their spelling.

MNEMONIC DEVICES

Whenever something in the meaning of a word is associated with something in the spelling of that word, you can use the meaning as a mnemonic device—as a reminder of how the word is to be spelled.

Several words with internal doubling have such clues to their spelling built into their meaning:

A *balloon,* with a double *l,* is often shaped like a *ball,* also with a double *l.*

A *fallacy,* with a double *l,* leads to a *fall,* also with a double *l,* in an argument.

The two *l*'s in *parallel* are themselves parallel, like railroad tracks.

Vaccines and *vaccinations* are administered in doses measured in *cc*'s.

Villains were earlier people who lived in *villages;* so both words have double *l*'s.

The stump on which you stubbed (double *b*) your toe was *stubborn* (double *b*).

If other words with internal doubling cause you trouble, you may be able to dream up such mnemonic devices as those to guide you in their spelling. If not, then you may have to rely upon a memorizing of their spellings one by one.

MEMORIZING

The number of individual spellings for you to memorize will no doubt be small, for comparatively few words are misspelled because of internal doubling. Also, you may master the spelling of some of these few with the help of word-building and mnemonic devices. And the remaining few can easily be memorized, especially if you use some of the aids suggested in Chapter 4.

Below is a list of words which are rather frequently misspelled because of a double letter inside them. Study the spelling of each word in the list, paying special attention to its doubling. Examine each word with the slow thoroughness suggested for proofreading (Chapter 1). If the doublings which you thus discover surprise you in the least—that is, seem the least bit unexpected or odd—put a mark by the word to indicate that you should study its spelling further, perhaps even memorizing it. Do that now, before reading on.

accommodate	fallacy	penicillin	territory
aggression	flammable	possess	terror
annual		possible	tobacco
	grammar		trellis
brilliant		rabbit	tyranny
bulletin	happiness	raccoon	
	horror	recommend	vaccine
carry			vacuum
challenge	intelligent	satellite	villain
confession		stubborn	
curriculum	narrative	succeed	
	necessary	success	
difference		sudden	
	occasion	syllable	
embarrass		symmetrical	
exaggerate	parallel		
excellent			

ANSWERS, EXERCISE 16

1. picnicking	11. bosses
2. shelved	12. frolicked
3. mottoes*	13. sopranos
4. twitches	14. chiefs
5. studios	15. colicky
6. axes	16. switches
7. gulches	17. rodeos
8. Romeos	18. mixes
9. searches	19. whizzes
10. commandos*	20. misses

If you got all answers right or marked the wrong ones as doubtful, go on to the next chapter. If not, review this chapter before taking the posttest.

*This is a competing spelling, discussed in Chapter 18.

After carefully studying those words, especially those with dou-blings that surprised you, do the next exercise.

EXERCISE 17

If needed, put a letter into the following blanks. If you are doubtful about your spelling, mark the "D" column.

		D			D
1.	a __ gression	____	9.	exce __ lent	____
2.	sate __ lite	____	10.	fla __ mable	____
3.	reco __ mend	____	11.	a __ nual	____
4.	penici __ lin	____	12.	te __ ror	____
5.	tre __ lis	____	13.	sy __ metrical	____
6.	acco __ modate	____	14.	cu __ riculum	____
7.	ho __ ror	____	15.	vi __ lain	____
8.	su __ den	____			

For answers see box on page 137.

POSTTEST 17

If needed, put a letter in the following blanks. If you are doubtful about your spelling, mark the "D" column.

		D			D
1.	po __ sible	____	6.	ra __ coon	____
2.	stu __ born	____	7.	nece __ sity	____
3.	emba __ rass	____	8.	po __ sess	____
4.	te __ ritory	____	9.	occa __ sion	____
5.	ra __ bit	____	10.	gra __ mar	____

For answers see box on page 139.

18

COMPETING SPELLINGS

PRETEST 18

If any letters are needed in the following blanks, insert them. If you are doubtful about a spelling, mark the "D" column.

D

1. He is our new neighb __ r. ____

2. That play has excellent dialog __ . ____

3. They drove thr __ out the entire night. ____

4. He is a person of high calib __ . ____

5. With her, conversation is a monolog __ . ____

6. He was accused of a misdemean __ r. ____

7. Some tough fib __ s are made of synthetics. ____

8. His judg __ ment is good. ____

9. That politician is a demagog __ . ____

10. All the col __ rs of the drapes were pastels. ____

For answers see box on page 141.

ANSWERS, POSTTEST 16

1. silos
2. relishes
3. cameos
4. falsettos
5. Jones's

6. panicking
7. cargoes*
8. leaves
9. belches
10. tomatoes

---

*This is a competing spelling, discussed in Chapter 18.

WHY SPELLINGS COMPETE

Far more than half the words now in English were not there a thousand years ago. They have come pouring in from foreign languages: French, Latin, Greek, and scores of others. When these words first arrived in English, they had the spelling of their earlier language, a foreign spelling, different from the one that a speaker of English would use. They were spelled, say, *philosophy* instead of *filosofy, Ouisconsin* instead of *Wisconsin, chateau* instead of *shato,* and *indices* instead of *indexes.* Later, as these incoming words became more firmly established in English, an "English" spelling developed for some of them and began to compete with the foreign spelling.

That competition between native and foreign spellings has turned out in every way that is theoretically possible. Sometimes, as in the case of *philosophy* and *chateau,* the foreign spelling has won. Sometimes, as in the case of *Wisconsin,* the native spelling has won. And sometimes, as in the case of *indices* and *indexes,* neither spelling has yet won a clear-cut victory. Both of those spellings, *indices* and *indexes,* are authorized by most recent dictionaries, with *indexes* preferred except for certain specialized scholarly uses.

In the past, competition has developed not only between a native and foreign spelling, but also between two native spellings. That happened about the time of the Revolutionary War and the War of 1812, when most Americans were hostile toward the British. Some colonists were so hostile that they wanted the language of America to be different from that of England. So, led by Noah Webster, they began using some different spellings: *honor* instead of *honour, meter* instead of *metre, judgment* instead of *judgement, jail* instead of *gaol, draftsman* instead of *draughtsman,* for example. At one time, therefore, it was possible for Americans to reveal their political loyalties by their spelling. Those who spelled *honor* without a *u* showed that they were Whigs, disloyal to George III; but those who spelled it with a *u* showed that they were Tories, loyal to the King. Most of these differences between American and British spelling persist to this day—a reason for continuing competition between spellings.

Competition also continues between traditional and simplified spellings, illustrated by *night* and *nite, though* and *tho, thorough* and *thoro, through* and *thru.* All dictionaries authorize the traditional spellings, and most include at least some of the simplified spellings, usually with a label like "informal" to warn that the spelling is not suitable for use in formal situations. Because the tests in this book are regarded as formal, only the traditional spellings are acceptable as answers.

In summary, competition continues between foreign and native, British and American, simplified and traditional spellings. Dictionaries still list two or more spellings for at least a thousand words, including *encyclopaedia* and *encyclopedia, grey* and *gray, memoranda* and *memorandums, theatre* and *theater,* and *thru* and *through.*

WHICH SPELLING IS RIGHT?

When a dictionary thus lists more than one spelling for a word, which spelling is right? Are all of them correct?

Well, all of them are used by a sizable and important group of people somewhere: *honor,* for example, by the Americans and *honour* by the British. So all of these variant spellings that are recorded in a dictionary have a claim to correctness somewhere, but they are not all regarded as equally correct everywhere. *Honor* is preferred in America; *honour* in Britain. Also *honor* is preferred in the English-language publications of the United Nations, no doubt because the international prestige of the United States is now greater than that of the United Kingdom. A later change in the comparative prestige of the two countries will probably bring about a corresponding change in the prestige of the two spellings.

How do dictionaries show which spelling is preferred? Most show it by giving it first in the main entry for the word. Thus *draftsman* is first in the main entry, while *draughtsman* is somewhere else. Where *draughtsman* will be found will be determined by which dictionary you happen to be using. It may follow *draftsman* immediately inside the main entry (*draftsman, draughtsman*). It may not be printed until near the end of the main entry, where it may be labeled "esp. Brit." Or it may be placed not in the main entry but in a secondary entry, elsewhere

ANSWERS, PRETEST 17

1. tyranny	6. parallel
2. fallacy	7. narrative
3. bulletin	8. intelligent
4. vaccine	9. vacuum
5. tobacco	10. exaggerate

If you got all answers right or marked the wrong ones as doubtful, go on to the next chapter. If not, study this chapter first.

in the alphabetical sequence of the words in the dictionary. In one dictionary, for example, the entry for *draftsman* comes just after the one for *drafthorse*, but the entry for *draughtsman* comes just after the one for *draughtboard*, on a later page in the dictionary. A main entry, which tells all about a word, normally runs for several lines, while a secondary entry, which may do no more than give the other spelling of the word, normally runs for only a line or so. Length thus shows whether an entry is main or secondary. Preferred spellings—let it be repeated for emphasis—are first in the main entry for a word. Unless you find a spelling in that position, you may be sure that it is not preferred.

RULES FOR PREFERRED SPELLINGS

Here are a half dozen rules for preferred spellings:

1. Prefer *or* to *our*. Thus *favor* to *favour*, *flavor* to *flavour*, *governor* to *governour*, *humor* to *humour*, *savior* to *saviour*, and *tumor* to *tumour*. But there is an exception: *glamour*.

2. Prefer *er* to *re*. Thus *caliber* to *calibre*, *center* to *centre*, *fiber* to *fibre*, *meter* to *metre*, and *theater* to *theatre*. (The competition between *theater* and *theatre* is still quite strong.)

3. Prefer *dgment* to *dgement*. Thus *abridgment* to *abridgement*, *acknowledgment* to *acknowledgement*, *judgment* to *judgement*, and *lodgment* to *lodgement*.

4. Prefer *ense* to *ence*. Thus *defense* to *defence*, *license* to *licence*, *offense* to *offence*, and *pretense* to *pretence*.

5. Prefer *logue* to *log*. Thus *analogue* to *analog*, *demagogue* to *demagog*, *dialogue* to *dialog*, *epilogue* to *epilog*, *monologue* to *monolog*, *pedagogue* to *pedagog*, *prologue* to *prolog*, and *synagogue* to *synagog*. But *catalog* is an exception, especially for librarians.

6. Prefer traditional to simplified spellings. Thus *night* to *nite*, *thorough* to *thoro*, *though* to *tho*, *through* to *thru*, and *tonight* to *tonite*.

In summary, prefer *or* to *our*, *er* to *re*, *dgment* to *dgement*, *ense* to *ence*, *logue* to *log*, and the traditional to the simplified spellings.

EXERCISE 18

If any letters are needed in the following blanks, insert them. If you are doubtful about a spelling, mark the "D" column.

D

1. She is full of preten ___ e.   ___

2. The new rabbi spoke at the synagog ___ .   ___

3. He has a wonderful sense of hum ___ r.   ___

4. Put a dime in the parking met ___ .   ___

5. That hat looks all ri ___ .   ___

6. Tho ___ he is ill, he will recover.   ___

7. Our football team is good on defen ___ .   ___

8. That book is an abridg ___ ment of an earlier   ___
   one.

9. Come over to my house toni ___ after supper.   ___

10. Of course we intended no offen ___ .   ___

11. A teacher may be a pedagog ___ .   ___

12. A new shopping cent ___ will soon open here.   ___

ANSWERS, EXERCISE 17

1. aggression	9. excellent
2. satellite	10. flammable
3. recommend	11. annual
4. penicillin	12. terror
5. trellis	13. symmetrical
6. accommodate	14. curriculum
7. horror	15. villain
8. sudden	

If you got all answers right or marked the wrong ones as doubtful, go on to the next chapter. If not, review this chapter before taking the posttest.

13. The surgeon removed a small tumo __ r.   ____

14. The trooper asked for my driver's licen __ e.   ____

15. At the end of a drama may be an epilog __ .   ____

16. An acknowledg __ ment of the letter was   ____
    needed.

17. That actress has real glamo __ r.   ____

18. This novel contains much dialog __ .   ____

19. He thinks lofty tho __ ts.   ____

20. The operation was an unexpected expen __ e.   ____

For answers see box on page 143.

POSTTEST 18

If any letters are needed in the following blanks, insert them. If you are
doubtful about a spelling, mark the "D" column.

        D

1. Finally we were thr __ with that dirty job!   ____

2. A dra __ tsman drew up plans for the project.   ____

3. We went to a theat __ on Broadway.   ____

4. Normandy was a lodg __ ment area for the Al-   ____
   lies.

5. We looked it up in an encyclop __ dia.   ____

6. The Confederate uniforms were gr __ y.   ____

7. He worked almost every n __ of the week.   ____

8. Whatever he does, he does thoro __ ly.   ____

9. Today a man read our gas met __ .   ____

10. The past is a prolog __ to the present.   ____

For answers see box on page 145.

19

COMPOUND WORDS

PRETEST 19

In the spaces provided, combine the italicized words. If you are doubtful about your combination, mark the "D" column.

	Combination	D
1. An *all out* effort	_____	___
2. a new *rain coat*	_____	___
3. a *high school* graduate	_____	___
4. a *light weight* sweater	_____	___
5. a *green horn* in town	_____	___
6. a *dog biscuit*	_____	___
7. a *middle class* family	_____	___
8. a vigorous *hand shake*	_____	___
9. does fancy *lace work*	_____	___
10. plays a *mouth organ*	_____	___

For answers see box on page 147.

ANSWERS, POSTTEST 17

1. possible	6. raccoon
2. stubborn	7. necessity
3. embarrass	8. possess
4. territory	9. occasion
5. rabbit	10. grammar

COMPOUND WORDS

Some words are built not merely by the addition of prefixes and suffixes to a stem, but by the joining together of whole words. Words formed in this way are called "compound words" and are illustrated by *horsewhip* and *pineapple*.

Such compound words are spelled, at one time or another, in four different ways. Sometimes they are written as two separate words *(red fox)*, sometimes as a hyphenated word *(red-hot)*, sometimes as a single word *(redhead)*, and sometimes as a single word, but with a change in the spelling of one of the combined words *(already)*. Of course the problem here is to decide how the combined whole words should be written—as two words, as a hyphenated word, as a single word, or as a single word with a changed spelling.

HYPHENATED WORDS

Hyphenation, as in *red-hot,* often depends upon how and where the combined words are used within a sentence. For instance, if the combined words are used as an adjective before a noun, they are hyphenated, as in "The red-hot stove gleamed in the dark room." But if the combined words, even though serving as an adjective, are not before a noun, they are not hyphenated, as in "The stove was red hot." In addition, there are a few other situations in which hyphenation is required—grammatical situations that are discussed more fully in a handbook of grammar than they should be in a guide to spelling. Thus a grammar handbook—not a dictionary—is of most help in hyphenating, for the dictionary makes no attempt to show all the situations in which hyphens are needed. Only handbooks do that.

Even so, dictionaries are sometimes responsible for an excessive use of hyphens. The fault is not with the dictionaries, but with users of dictionaries who do not recognize the difference between a hyphen and a centered period—a special mark rarely found outside a dictionary. Here is an example of the two marks:

great-grand·child.

The hyphen is between *great* and *grand,* while the centered period is between *grand* and *child.* If you look up that word in your own dictionary, you will probably never again confuse those two marks—that is, never again mistakenly put in a hyphen where your dictionary has a centered period.

Dictionaries use centered periods to show where a word may properly be broken at the end of a line, as a marker of the boundary between two syllables in a word. That is why if you open your dictionary anywhere and start looking for centered periods, you will probably find many of them, especially in words with three or more syllables. (In words with just two syllables, the boundaries between syllables are normally signaled by accent marks, not centered periods.)

In general, then, the only time you should put a hyphen where a dictionary has a centered period is when you break a word at the end of a line.

Of course you should hyphenate where your dictionary does—for example, in such words as *co-op, co-owner, great-grandchild*, and *light-years*. Also, you should rely upon a healthy sense of doubt to lead you to the dictionary for the hyphenations authorized there.

SEPARATED AND FUSED WORDS

A dictionary is also the final authority for separating words *(red fox)* or for fusing them together *(redhead)*. It is reliable, but utterly inconsistent. These combinations of words are so tricky, so unpredictable, that almost everybody has to look up at least some of them. You will see why when you contrast *dewdrop* with *dew line, horsepower* with *horse sense, keyhole* with *key ring, photoflash* with *photo finish, rainstorm* with *rain water*, and *scatterbrain* with *scatter rug*. There is no consistency here, no rule, no short cut. Either you must memorize the spelling of such words, or you must get the habit of looking them up in your dictionary. There is no other way.

COMBINED WORDS WITH CHANGED SPELLINGS

Finally, consider the words like *already*, which are formed by the combination of two whole words *(all* and *ready)*, are written as a single word, but have a change in the spelling of one of the combined words

ANSWERS, PRETEST 18

1. neighbor
2. dialogue
3. throughout
4. caliber
5. monologue
6. misdemeanor
7. fibers
8. judgment
9. demagogue
10. colors

If all your answers were right or if you marked all wrong ones as doubtful, go directly to the next pretest. If not, study this chapter first.

(*al* for *all*). Many of the most common words in the language belong in this group: *always* (not *allways*), *fulfill* (not *fullfill*), *hateful* (not *hatefull*), *pastime* (not *passtime*), *until* (not *untill*), *welcome* (not *wellcome*), and *wherever* (not *whereever*). In all these combinations, the meaning of at least one of the words has been changed or weakened. Thus the combination does not mean exactly what the two words would mean if used adjacent to each other. *Always* does not mean the same as *all ways*; *fulfill* does not mean the same as *fill full*; and so on.

Only rarely are these common combinations of words misspelled; but another combination, which resembles them in some ways, is misspelled quite often: *all right*. That combination is not like *almost, already, although,* and *always*. Instead it has two separate words, both of them spelled out fully, with white space conspicuous between them.

EXERCISE 19

In the spaces provided, combine the italicized words. If you are doubtful about your combination, mark the "D" column.

	Combination	D
1. Here is an *up to the minute* report.	_____	____
2. Tonight we may get a *thunder storm*.	_____	____
3. Always he arrives with an *on the dot* promptness.	_____	____
4. What she says is *on the level*.	_____	____
5. That *farm house* has been abandoned.	_____	____
6. Too often on the voyage he was *sea sick*.	_____	____
7. Clifford will be here *in a minute*.	_____	____
8. The vending machine did not give the *quarter back*.	_____	____
9. What the football coach prayed for was a good *quarter back*.	_____	____
10. First the hired man cut the grass in the *front yard*.	_____	____

11. The captain of the tennis team had a good *back hand.* _____ ____

12. Our dog stayed in the fenced *back yard.* _____ ____

13. Lincoln often wore a *stove pipe* hat. _____ ____

14. The rejected suitor had a *down at the mouth* look. _____ ____

15. Finally the jet came *down at the airport.* _____ ____

16. The atmosphere in the room was that of a *just before the storm* calm. _____ ____

17. Of course every medical doctor is *college trained.* _____ ____

18. The plane landed *just before the storm.* _____ ____

19. Royster is an *up and coming* young executive. _____ ____

20. *College trained* young men get jobs rather easily today. _____ ____

For answers see box on page 149.

For answers see box on page 149.

ANSWERS, EXERCISE 18

1. pretense	11. pedagogue
2. synagogue	12. center
3. humor	13. tumor
4. meter	14. license
5. right	15. epilogue
6. though	16. acknowledgment
7. defense	17. glamour
8. abridgment	18. dialogue
9. tonight	19. thoughts
10. offense	20. expense

If all the answers you missed were marked "D," go on to the next chapter.

POSTTEST 19

Combine the italicized words in the spaces provided. If you are doubtful about your spelling, mark the "D" column.

	Combination	D
1. a *green light* for us	_____	____
2. at Lewis *High School*	_____	____
3. a *dog house*	_____	____
4. take a *rain check*	_____	____
5. ten *light years* away	_____	____
6. several *hand grenades*	_____	____
7. served as a *middle man*	_____	____
8. another *lace pillow*	_____	____
9. cleaned the *mouth piece*	_____	____
10. an old *hand me down*	_____	____

For answers see box on page 151.

APPENDIXES

ANSWERS, POSTTEST 18

1. through
2. draftsman
3. theater
4. lodgment
5. encyclopedia

6. gray
7. night
8. thoroughly
9. meter
10. prologue

TAKING THE
DIAGNOSTIC TEST

Although there are many different causes of misspelling, you do not have to contend with all of them. Most people have trouble with only a few, and the diagnostic test which you are about to take will show you the few on which you need to work. By concentrating on the few actually causing you trouble, you may achieve the greatest improvement with the least work.

TAKING THE TEST

PART ONE

In each of the following 104 expressions is a word with a blank in it. Put into that blank whatever is needed to complete the spelling of the word. If nothing is needed, do not add anything.

   If you are not sure how to spell a word, try to spell it anyhow. Then mark the "D" space by the word to show that you are doubtful about its spelling. Later you will be told how to mark the "I" and "C" spaces by each word.

	D	I	C
1. She will d __ vorce her husband.	__	__	__
2. Was it enviro __ ment or heredity?	__	__	__
3. More __ migrants left Italy daily.	__	__	__
4. What did he advi __ e you to do?	__	__	__
5. What misch __ vous boys!	__	__	__
6. Buy prefer __ ed stocks.	__	__	__
7. Which method is he us __ ing?	__	__	__
8. A __ point a committee.	__	__	__
9. He was charged with drunken __ ess.	__	__	__

	D	**I**	**C**
10. He is stud __ ing to be a doctor.	___	___	___
11. The son mimic __ ed his father.	___	___	___
12. She bought a vacu __ m cleaner.	___	___	___
13. He wrote many memorand __ .	___	___	___
14. Do not d __ spair; he will return.	___	___	___
15. Toys fas __ inate children.	___	___	___
16. Order some new station __ ry.	___	___	___
17. Bath __ the dog once a week.	___	___	___
18. In baseball he played left f __ ld.	___	___	___
19. She excel __ ed in art.	___	___	___
20. Stop rac __ ing your motor.	___	___	___
21. What did the teacher a __ sign?	___	___	___
22. The letter was mi __ sent. (Sent wrong.)	___	___	___
23. This food satisf __ s me completely.	___	___	___
24. Our cow gave birth to twin cal __ s.	___	___	___
25. That was a dif __ icult decision.	___	___	___
26. Use your best judg __ ment.	___	___	___
27. The storm caused much d __ struction.	___	___	___
28. Send it to the chemistry lab __ tory.	___	___	___

ANSWERS, PRETEST 19

1. all-out
2. raincoat
3. high-school
4. lightweight
5. greenhorn
6. dog biscuit
7. middle-class
8. handshake
9. lacework
10. mouth organ

If you missed no answers here, skip this chapter.

	D	I	C

29. The Indians held a coun __ l of war.

30. Cotton has the power of absor __ tion.

31. He is not religious; he is an ath __ st.

32 That was a compel __ ing reason.

33. It is extrem __ ly important.

34. She was an i __ literate old woman.

35. He was u __ noticed in the crowd.

36. She appl __ s for too many jobs.

37. The soprano __ s sang quite well.

38. This is unexplored ter __ itory.

39. The pie has a fine flavo __ r.

40. They are in the same cat __ gory.

41. His hobby is mini __ ture trains.

42. Say something compl __ mentary.

43. Alabama se __ ed from the Union.

44. What grade did you rec __ ve?

45. Plan __ ing the party was fun.

46. She is always quot __ ing from the Bible.

47. Do not su __ press the truth.

48. Poor diet caused his thin __ ess.

49. Attorn __ s practice law.

50. Pass me the potato __ s, please.

51. You exag __ erate too much.

52. They went to a movie theat __ .

53. She has too much opt __ mism.

54. It came by special deliv __ ry.

55. He was a man of high princip __ s.

56. The new model super __ ed the old.
(Took the place of.)

	D	I	C
57. To be egotistic is to be conc __ ted.	——	——	——
58. She has a win __ ing personality.	——	——	——
59. This result is notic __ ably better.	——	——	——
60. They added an a __ nex to their house.	——	——	——
61. This is an ove __ rated novel.	——	——	——
62. The monk __ s at the zoo amused us.	——	——	——
63. We have picnic __ ed here before.	——	——	——
64. There is a good vac __ ine for smallpox.	——	——	——
65. Is his new suit blue or gr __ y?	——	——	——
66. Rep __ tition helps learning.	——	——	——
67. They crossed the northern bound __ ry.	——	——	——
68. Who __ hat is that?	——	——	——
69. The news stories were cens __ red.	——	——	——
70. He used dec __ t to fool us.	——	——	——

ANSWERS, EXERCISE 19

1. up-to-the-minute
2. thunderstorm
3. on-the-dot
4. on the level
5. farmhouse
6. seasick
7. in a minute
8. quarter back
9. quarterback
10. front yard
11. backhand
12. back yard
13. stovepipe
14. down-at-the-mouth
15. down at the airport
16. just-before-the-storm
17. college trained
18. just before the storm
19. up-and-coming
20. College-trained

If all the answers which you missed were marked "D," go to the next chapter. If not, review this chapter before taking the posttest.

	D	**I**	**C**
71. This is the hot __ est day yet.	___	___	___
72. The car is in servic __ able condition.	___	___	___
73. The President has an i __ mense job.	___	___	___
74. That is real __ y the truth.	___	___	___
75. We are suppl __ ing you the best.	___	___	___
76. She has sung many solo __ s.	___	___	___
77. He is as stub __ orn as a mule.	___	___	___
78. This gun has a small calib __ .	___	___	___
79. It was an incred __ ble accident.	___	___	___
80. Joe and Louise use __ to be friends.	___	___	___
81. He is an __ minent preacher.	___	___	___
82. She works in the person __ l office.	___	___	___
83. He's at the h __ ght of his career.	___	___	___
84. His prefer __ ence is tea.	___	___	___
85. It was a gorg __ ous sunset.	___	___	___
86. Su __ port at least one charity.	___	___	___
87. She smiled cool __ y at him.	___	___	___
88. Her story mystif __ s me.	___	___	___
89. We heard echo __ s in the canyon.	___	___	___
90. He is addicted to tobac __ o.	___	___	___
91. She has no sense of humo __ r.	___	___	___
92. Coffee is a mild stimul __ nt.	___	___	___
93. He was a three-letter ath __ lete.	___	___	___
94. The kitten hurt it __ paw.	___	___	___
95. How will that decision __ ffect you?	___	___	___
96. Eat enough prot __ ns every day.	___	___	___
97. Show defer __ ence for authority.	___	___	___
98. A car __ ful study of that is needed.	___	___	___
99. He o __ poses everything.	___	___	___

	D	I	C
100. Its sudden ___ ess surprised us.	___	___	___
101. The store has many variet ___ s.	___	___	___
102. They own two piano ___ s.	___	___	___
103. What he said embar ___ assed us.	___	___	___
104. The new catalog ___ has arrived.	___	___	___

PART TWO

The following expressions should be written (A) as one word, (B) as a hyphenated word, or (c) as separate words. Mark the appropriate space (A, B, or C) by each expression. If you are doubtful about a spelling, mark the "D" space, too.

	A	B	C	D
1. head on (collision)	___	___	___	___
2. post office	___	___	___	___
3. dew point	___	___	___	___
4. weather map	___	___	___	___
5. all right	___	___	___	___
6. hand to mouth	___	___	___	___
7. head waiter	___	___	___	___
8. post master	___	___	___	___

MARKING THE TEST

In the box on the next page are the answers for the test. As you compare your answers with those, mark the "I" (for "incorrect") space by every word which you misspelled. Do that now, before reading on.

The misspellings on your test were probably the result of carelessness or of ignorance. Carelessness was the villain if you failed to get on the paper what you had in your mind as the spelling of the word—if, for example, you failed to cross a *t* or to dot an *i*. To find out how many of your misspellings were caused by carelessness, look again at each word now marked "I" on the test. If the mistake was caused only by an unintentional slip of the pen, put a mark in the "C" (for "careless") column by that word. Do it now, before reading further.

TABULATING THE RESULTS

Your performance on the test can best be measured and analyzed after you have filled out the spelling profile (on page 154) and then the tabulation of totals (on page 155). The profile and the tabulation will make each of your problems stand out clearly, for quick identification, and will guide you in what you need to do to improve your spelling.

THE PROFILE

How the profile can help you will be obvious when you understand how it and the test underlying it have been constructed. Several words scattered throughout the test involve a single problem. The numbers representing those words are assembled in a single horizontal line on the profile. Therefore, when you mark on the profile the numbers of the words that you got wrong on the test, you can see immediately how many words involving each kind of problem you missed.

In more detail, each horizontal row of numbers on the left of the profile represents a different problem in spelling. Thus the top row (1, 14, 27, 40, 53, 66, 79, 92) represents a single problem, "unstressed vowels," which is named in the column in the center of the profile. Toward the right, the next column gives the number of the chapter dealing with that problem, a chapter which may help you to solve it. At the extreme right are columns where you may tabulate, for each of the problems in spelling, the totals of the numbers of the words that you missed and that you earlier were doubtful about.

When other horizontal rows of numbers on the left of the profile are marked, they will lead you in the same way to the identification of your problem, near the center of the profile, and then, on the right, to

ANSWERS, DIAGNOSTIC TEST
PART ONE

1. divorce
2. environment
3. emigrants
4. advise
5. mischievous
6. preferred
7. using
8. appoint
9. drunkenness
10. studying
11. mimicked
12. vacuum
13. memorandums
14. despair
15. fascinate
16. stationery
17. bathe
18. field
19. excelled
20. racing
21. assign
22. missent
23. satisfies
24. calves
25. difficult
26. judgment
27. destruction
28. laboratory
29. council
30. absorption
31. atheist
32. compelling
33. extremely
34. illiterate
35. unnoticed

36. applies
37. sopranos
38. territory
39. flavor
40. category
41. miniature
42. complimentary
43. seceded
44. receive
45. planning
46. quoting
47. suppress
48. thinness
49. attorneys
50. potatoes
51. exaggerate
52. theater
53. optimism
54. delivery
55. principles
56. superseded
57. conceited
58. winning
59. noticeably
60. annex
61. overrated
62. monkeys
63. picnicked
64. vaccine
65. gray
66. repetition
67. boundary
68. whose
69. censored

70. deceit
71. hottest
72. serviceable
73. immense
74. really
75. supplying
76. solos
77. stubborn
78. caliber
79. incredible
80. used
81. eminent
82. personnel
83. height
84. preference
85. gorgeous
86. support
87. coolly
88. mystifies
89. echoes
90. tobacco
91. humor
92. stimulant
93. athlete
94. its
95. affect
96. proteins
97. deference
98. careful
99. oppose
100. suddenness
101. varieties
102. pianos
103. embarrassed
104. catalog

PART TWO

1. B	3. C	5. C	7. A
2. C	4. C	6. B	8. A

THE PROFILE

Item Number								Name of Problem	Chapter Number	Total Missed	Total Doubted
Part one											
1	14	27	40	53	66	79	92	Unstressed vowels	5	___	___
2	15	28	41	54	67	80	93	Omitted and added letters	6,7	___	___
3	16	29	42	55	68	81	94	Identical pronunciations	8	___	___
4	17	30	43	56	69	82	95	Similar pronunciations	9	___	___
5	18	31	44	57	70	83	96	IE or EI	10	___	___
6	19	32	45	58	71	84	97	Final doubling	11	___	___
7	20	33	46	59	72	85	98	Final E	12	___	___
8	21	34	47	60	73	86	99	Assimilative doubling	13	___	___
9	22	35	48	61	74	87	100	Additive doubling	14	___	___
10	23	36	49	62	75	88	101	Final Y	15	___	___
11	24	37	50	63	76	89	102	Other final letters	16	___	___
12	25	38	51	64	77	90	103	Internal doubling	17	___	___
13	26	39	52	65	78	91	104	Competing spellings	18	___	___
Part Two											
1	2	3	4	5	6	7	8	Compound words	19	___	___

the number of the chapter that deals with that problem. In addition, the "Total" columns near the right will show you approximately how much trouble each problem has caused you: a great deal, a little, or none. So the filled-out profile will reveal which parts of the book you should study much, a little, or not at all.

Now you should mark the profile according to these instructions:

1. In the column headed "Item Number," draw a line through the number of every word that you missed on the test.

2. In addition, put a circle around the number of every word whose spelling you have already marked "D" (for "doubtful"). A row on the profile may then look like this, with some numbers unmarked, some circled, some lined, and some circled and lined:

1   (14)   <s>27</s>   40   (<s>53</s>)

3 Fill in both "Total" columns on the right of the profile.

Do these things now, before reading further.

THE TABULATION OF TOTALS

Although your profile will show many of your strengths and weaknesses as a speller, the diagnosis cannot be completed until you have also filled in the following tabulation of totals. Fill in that tabulation now, getting your information by counting the marks already put on the profile or on the test sheets themselves.

1. Total number of words lined or marked "I" (for "incorrect") ___

2. Total circled or marked "D" (for "doubtful") ___

3. Total marked both "I" and "D," thus:

D   I   C   or   (<s>53</s>)
✓ ✓ ___
___

4. Total marked "I," but not "D"
   Subtract the number in line 3, above, from that in line 1, above. ___

5. Total marked "D," but not "I"
   Subtract the number in line 3 from that in line 2. ___

6. Total marked "C" (for "careless")
   Count the number marked "C" on your test sheets. ___

7. Total marked "I," but not "D" or "C"
   Add the numbers in lines 3 and 6. Then subtract that total
   from the number in line 1. Enter the result here: ____

8. Total marked "I" and "D" or "C"
   Subtract the number in line 7 from that in line 1. ____

NOTE: In the next appendix you may compare your performance on this test with the performance of a hundred freshmen in college.

B
INTERPRETING
THE TEST

What, according to the diagnostic test, are your problems in spelling? The profile, when properly interpreted, will show you some of your problems; and the tabulation of totals will reveal others. Consider first what the profile shows.

INTERPRETING THE PROFILE

The profile shows at a glance which verbal problems in spelling are causing you no trouble, which are causing some, and which are causing most. In more detail, if no number in a row is lined, you may assume that you do not have the problem represented by that row. If only one number in a row is lined, you may assume that you do have the designated problem, but only to a limited extent—that is why a quick reading of the appropriate chapter may be sufficient to enable you to solve the problem. On the other hand, if several numbers in a row are lined, then the problem represented by the row is probably a serious one for you—serious enough to require that you study the appropriate chapter carefully, perhaps even repeatedly, until you are a thorough master of its contents.

For your convenience, spaces are provided in the next appendix for you to jot down the numbers of the chapters that, according to the profile, you should study. Also there are spaces where you can check off the completion of each of the chapters thus assigned in this highly individualized program of work.

INTERPRETING THE TABULATION

Each item in the tabulation (pages 155-156) shows something about your strengths and weaknesses as a speller. Below is an item-by-item report on how a hundred college freshmen, using a version of the diagnostic test in an earlier edition of this book, scored on their tabulation. If you compare your own scores with theirs, you will get some idea of how your own strengths and weaknesses as a speller compare with theirs.

1. Total Number of Words Marked "I" (for "Incorrect").   Every college freshman who took the test missed at least four words, and one missed sixty-one. The top quarter of these students missed from four to eighteen words; the bottom quarter, from thirty-five to sixty-one; and the middle half, from nineteen to thirty-four. Where do you rank among these students?

2. Total Marked "D" (for "Doubtful").   This is the number of spellings that you were not sure of, that you presumably would have looked up in a dictionary if you had been permitted to use a dictionary on the test. Thus your score here shows whether you are so sure of your spellings that you rarely consult a dictionary—or so unsure that you may often consult a dictionary.

A score of zero here indicates an excessive sureness, an unwarranted cockiness, or an overconfidence in your ability to spell. Twenty-four of the freshmen who took the test had a zero here, although all of them misspelled at least a few words, and several misspelled many. Half the freshmen marked only one, two, or three of their spellings as doubtful, although all these students missed a dozen or even dozens of words. In brief, most students were grossly overconfident about their ability to spell—a serious personal flaw for people who want to avoid misspellings in what they write.

But not all the students were deficient in their sense of doubt. One was doubtful about a total of thirty-four of his spellings, and others were doubtful about sizable numbers of their spellings. They showed how a big, healthy sense of doubt—if used with the aid of a dictionary—can greatly reduce the number of misspellings in their work. For you, too, an increased sense of doubt may lead to a dramatic decrease in the number of your misspellings.

3. Total Marked Both "I" and "D."   One student marked nineteen of his misspelled words as doubtful spellings—an indication of how much good an active sense of doubt can do. With the aid of a dictionary, he would have avoided nineteen misspellings on the test—a number big enough to make the difference between succeeding and failing in most situations.

In contrast, about a third of the students did not mark any of their misspellings as doubtful. They obviously would have misspelled the same number of words even if a dictionary had been within easy reach when they took the test. Their overconfidence led, inevitably, to underachievement.

Reassuringly, two-thirds of the students marked as doubtful at least some of their misspellings. This fact shows that most people have at least the beginnings of a sense of doubt—a sense of doubt that, if nurtured and encouraged to grow, can bring about a dramatic reduction in the number of words actually misspelled.

Can an increased sense of doubt help you?

4. Total Marked "I," but not "D."   This number is a measure of your overconfidence as a speller, for it shows how often you thought that your spellings were right when, actually, they were wrong. It shows how much or how little your sense of doubt needs to be increased if you are going to use doubtfulness as an aid to achievement.

One student was doubtful about all his misspellings except one. He had only a negligible amount of overconfidence. With a dictionary at hand, he would rarely if ever misspell a word—a major accomplishment. He had a sense of doubt that was just about ideal.

At the other end of the scale were two freshman who misspelled forty-nine words that were not marked as doubtful. These two freshmen obviously had far more overconfidence than was good for them. Indeed, overconfidence was probably the chief reason for their poor performance on the test and, perhaps, in whatever they wrote.

These scores, ranging from one to forty-nine, show that different people have different degrees of overconfidence. Do you now have a large or small degree of overconfidence?

5. Total Marked "D," but Not "I."   This number shows how reliable—or how unreliable—your sense of doubt is. It is totally reliable if you score zero. The zero reveals that you actually misspelled every word that you, as you took the test, marked as doubtful. But if every word that you marked doubtful was actually spelled right, then your sense of doubt is totally unreliable.

A fourth of the students who earlier took the test had a zero here. So their sense of doubt was totally reliable on the test. They would have avoided a misspelling if, every time that they marked a word as doubtful, they had looked it up in their dictionary.

Another fourth of the students had a score of one here. So their sense of doubt was almost totally reliable. If they had consulted their dictionary for the spellings that they were doubtful about, they, too, would have avoided a large number of misspellings. They would have discovered that only one of the spellings that they doubted was actually right.

In brief, half the students had a score of zero or one; half had a sense of doubt that was totally—or almost totally—reliable. Three-fourths of the students had a score of seven or below; and almost all the students, when they marked a word as doubtful, were far more likely to spell it wrong than right.

These statistics show that the sense of doubt is surprisingly reliable for most people. With surprising frequency it signals that a word may be about to be misspelled when, as a matter of fact, it *is* about to be misspelled. In effect, it can serve as a red light, signaling that you should stop and consult your dictionary. The statistical odds are very high that such stops will save you far more trouble than they cause.

6. Total Marked "C" (for "Careless"). The tested students made very few careless errors. Half reported none, and others reported only a few. Obviously most of these students—simply because they were taking a test—were more careful than they normally are when they are writing hurriedly and with no special attention to spelling. Thus the score here is not a particularly reliable indication of how careless or how careful you are in your writing.

But you know, if you think honestly about it, how you rate on a scale that ranges from utter carelessness, at one extreme, to meticulous carefulness, at the other. If you cannot give yourself a grade of a hundred in meticulous carefulness, then you should rely heavily upon a proof-reading of your work, as described in Chapter 1. Indeed, such proof-reading may be the only hope for the careless.

7. Total Marked "I," but Not "D" or "C." This is the number of words that you would still have misspelled if you had done only two things: if you had consulted your dictionary for every spelling that you were doubtful about and if you had proofread your work to eliminate careless misspellings. If the number here, for 7, is appreciably lower than the number for 1, then doubtfulness and proofreading can be of great help to you in improving your spelling, even without an increase in your sense of doubt and in your skill in proofreading. With a large increase in these two things, your improvement may be far greater.

Of the students who took the test earlier, one made a perfect score here: zero. Every word this student misspelled was marked either "D" or "C." Another student misspelled only one word that she did not mark as "D" or "C"—an almost perfect score. These two students demonstrate how much good can be accomplished by a sharp sense of doubt and by careful proofreading.

But other students got nowhere close to perfection. One scored forty-four rather than zero. Another scored forty-three. Indeed, twenty-five of the hundred students scored between twenty-eight and forty-four. These students are the ones who would benefit the most by increasing their sense of doubt and by whetting their skill in proofreading. They need—badly—to do those two things. Do you?

8. Total Marked "I" and "D" or "C."   This is the number of misspellings that you might have avoided by consulting your dictionary about doubtful words and by careful proofreading. By doing these two things, one student tested earlier would have avoided twenty-seven misspellings—an impressive number. Twenty-five of the students would have avoided from fifteen to twenty-seven misspellings—also an impressive number. Such statistics show that a great deal may be accomplished by doubting and by proofreading. That is why many chapters of this book have been designed to help you to increase these two valuable skills in spelling.

C
PLANNING YOUR PROGRAM

Your program of study should have two main stages. In the first you should seek to solve the personal problems which affect your spelling, including such problems as carelessness and overconfidence in spelling. In the second you should seek to solve the verbal problems, including such problems as choosing between *ie* and *ei* in spellings.

THE FIRST STAGE

The personal problems affecting your spelling should be solved at the very beginning, before you attempt to deal with the verbal problems, because the solution of some of the verbal problems depends upon the earlier solution of the personal problems. In some instances you may not have the tools for dealing with the verbal problems until you get the personal problems under control. It is a good idea to get a hammer before trying to drive a nail.

The first four chapters of the book, which form Part One, deal with the personal problems and provide you with some tools for working with the verbal problems. That is why you should begin by a study of these chapters, especially if you do not make a perfect score on the pretests for these chapters. Your assignment for the first stage is therefore this:

Study	Completed
Chapter 1	____
Chapter 2	____
Chapter 3	____
Chapter 4	____

Mark each chapter above as you complete it—to keep an up-to-date record of what you have done and what remains for you to do.

THE SECOND STAGE

In the second stage you will work one by one on the verbal problems revealed by the profile of your performance on the diagnostic test. Below is a tabulation of the possible assignments for this second stage. With the help of the profile on page 154, mark the "To Do" space by each chapter which, according to the profile, you should study. Then, as you complete each of the assigned chapters, mark it in the "Done" space— again so that you may have an up-to-date record of what you have done and what remains for you to do.

	Row	Chapter	To Do	Done
Part one	1	5	——	——
	2	6, 7	——	——
	3	8	——	——
	4	9	——	——
	5	10	——	——
	6	11	——	——
	7	12	——	——
	8	13	——	——
	9	14	——	——
	10	15	——	——
	11	16	——	——
	12	17	——	——
	13	18	——	——
Part Two		19	——	——

When the "To Do" column of that tabulation of assignments has been filled in, you have a panoramic view of the program of study ahead of you. Because later chapters sometimes build upon information provided in earlier chapters, it is strongly recommended that you work with these chapters in numerical order—for example, beginning with Chapter 5 (if it is marked in the "To Do" column) and ending with Chapter 19 (if it is marked).

Begin your program of study for improvement now, starting with the first stage and continuing on through the second.

FINAL TEST

This final test is intended for use after instruction has been completed, especially if the instruction was preceded by the diagnostic test in Appendix A. The diagnostic and final tests have the same design, with samples of eight words for each of fourteen trouble spots in spelling; but the words themselves in the two tests are, for the most part, different. A comparison of the performance on the two tests therefore reveals not whether you have learned to spell certain words, but whether you have learned to deal successfully with fourteen (or fewer) trouble spots in spelling. A comparison of the performance on the two tests may also reveal something else which is very important: how much your sense of doubt has been increased by work with the book.

TAKING THE TEST

PART ONE

In each of the following 104 expressions is a word with a blank in it. Put into the blank whatever is needed to complete the spelling of the word. If nothing is needed, do not add anything.

If you are not sure how to spell a word, try to spell it anyhow. Then mark the "D" space by the word to show that you are doubtful about its spelling. Later you will be told how to mark the "I" and "C" spaces by each word.

	D	I	C
1. She d __ spises spiders.	___	___	___
2. Ac __ uracy is important.	___	___	___
3. Our ancestors were im __ igrants to Iowa.	___	___	___
4. She writes advi __ e for the lovelorn.	___	___	___
5. That fr __ ght train derailed.	___	___	___
6. The pitcher fan __ ed all three batters.	___	___	___
7. We ate in the din __ ing room.	___	___	___

	D	I	C

8. Su __ port your church regularly.

9. The prodigal mi __ spent a fortune.

10. T __ ing shoestrings is difficult for him.

11. We enjoy the melod __ s of Bach.

12. The heat in August is ter __ ible.

13. This is an abridg __ ment of a big dictionary.

14. They wanted to d __ scover a cure for cancer.

15. He craved the lux __ ry of sleeping late

16. The train was station __ ry.

17. We put up a bath __ for the birds.

18. We had to choose among a var __ ty of styles.

19. He tried to conceal his thin __ ing hair.

20. He's always on the fir __ ing line.

21. Socrates did not co __ rupt morals.

22. She spoke in an un __ atural tone of voice.

23. That noise signif __ s nothing.

24. She buys antique cameo __ s.

25. That is a dif __ icult decision to make.

26. He was happy tho __ tired.

27 The rain will soon d __ minish.

28. They raised a large fam __ ily.

29. The lawyer gave good coun __ l.

30. Cotton will absor __ water.

31. Zeus was a Greek d __ ty.

	D	I	C

32. He's the big __ est liar in town.   ___ ___ ___

33. Those losses are trac __ able to him.   ___ ___ ___

34. He made an a __ peal to reason.   ___ ___ ___

35. The twins are di __ similar.   ___ ___ ___

36. This lens magnif __ s wonderfully.   ___ ___ ___

37. The plural of *elf* is *el __ s.*   ___ ___ ___

38. Railroad tracks are paral __ el.   ___ ___ ___

39. Does he favo __ r his father?   ___ ___ ___

40. The maint __ nance of a car is expensive.   ___ ___ ___

41. Vote for good gover __ ment.   ___ ___ ___

42. Those colors compl __ ment each other.   ___ ___ ___

43. He devi __ ed a new plan for sales.   ___ ___ ___

44. Do not gr __ ve for the dead.   ___ ___ ___

45. He was transfer __ ed to another city.   ___ ___ ___

46. That is a manag __ able load to carry.   ___ ___ ___

47. Do capitalists o __ press the poor?   ___ ___ ___

48. He was smiling evil __ y at her.   ___ ___ ___

49. The orchestra played medl __ s of hit songs.   ___ ___ ___

50. He was caught traffic __ ing in drugs.   ___ ___ ___

51. She showed the fal __ acy in his reasoning.   ___ ___ ___

52. A met __ is a little more than a yard.   ___ ___ ___

53. That's just Russian prop __ ganda.   ___ ___ ___

54. Investigate before you condem __ .   ___ ___ ___

55. You are al __ together wrong.   ___ ___ ___

56. Ladies pr __ ce __ d __ gentlemen.   ___ ___ ___

57. Start with a clean p __ ce of paper.   ___ ___ ___

	D	I	C
58. We concur __ ed with the boss quickly.	__	__	__
59. The plan was du __ ly approved.	__	__	__
60. Then he became i __ rational.	__	__	__
61. He treated his enemies cruel __ y.	__	__	__
62. He carr __ s a tune carefully, fearfully.	__	__	__
63. First the commando __ s landed.	__	__	__
64. He elaborated on the hor __ ors of war.	__	__	__
65. Listen to the clamo __ r of that mob!	__	__	__
66. The troops advanced with compar __ tive ease.	__	__	__
67. We have a big su __ prise for you!	__	__	__
68. His arrival is im __ inent.	__	__	__
69. The new often super __ des the old.	__	__	__
70. We hated to forf __ t the game.	__	__	__
71. The train travel __ ed at high speed.	__	__	__
72. I love you tru __ ly.	__	__	__
73. But that would be im __ oral!	__	__	__
74. I met him social __ y.	__	__	__
75. She is one of the lovel __ s in the chorus.	__	__	__
76. We saw angels with halo __ s.	__	__	__
77. The doctors vac __ inated everybody.	__	__	__
78. These tough fib __ s are for tires.	__	__	__
79. She had a defi __ nt attitude.	__	__	__
80. We tried to sof __ en the blow.	__	__	__
81. A quart is a fo __ rth of a gallon.	__	__	__
82. He was a statesman of great statu __ e.	__	__	__
83. They built a sh __ ld against the attack.	__	__	__

	D	I	C
84. We defer __ ed the payment of the bill.	__	__	__
85. The senators spoke grav __ ly about it.	__	__	__
86. What an o __ riginal idea!	__	__	__
87. They were di __ satisfied with their purchase.	__	__	__
88. Little jock __ s make big money.	__	__	__
89. She is always quoting motto __ s.	__	__	__
90. What a dif __ erence money can make!	__	__	__
91. Rain continued all thr __ the night.	__	__	__
92. Who will spons __ r that program?	__	__	__
93. We had pum __ kin pie for dessert.	__	__	__
94. The __ is a skunk outside.	__	__	__
95. They pr __ c __ ded on their trip.	__	__	__
96. He tried to dec __ ve everybody.	__	__	__
97. The teacher quiz __ ed the class.	__	__	__
98. That beer is a case of good judg __ ment.	__	__	__
99. Her behavior is too i __ mature.	__	__	__
100. Congress will ove __ ride the veto.	__	__	__
101. We had only the necessit __ s of life.	__	__	__
102. Those tankers carried cargo __ s of oil.	__	__	__
103. They fought the tyran __ y of a dictator.	__	__	__
104. The dialog __ in the play is sprightly.	__	__	__

PART TWO

The following expressions should be written (A) as one word, (B) as a hyphenated word, or (C) as separate words. Mark the appropriate space (A, B, or C) by each expression. If you are doubtful about a spelling, mark the "D" space, too.

	A	B	C	D
1. He's a *good natured* fellow.	——	——	——	——
2. The storm followed the *sea coast*.	——	——	——	——
3. Don't be so *down cast*.	——	——	——	——
4. Enjoy the *sea breeze*.	——	——	——	——
5. He did a quick *double take*.	——	——	——	——
6. She has a very *good nature*.	——	——	——	——
7. Legislators are *law makers*.	——	——	——	——
8. The *down payment* is small.	——	——	——	——

MARKING THE TEST

The answers for the test are in the box on page 171. As you compare your answers with those, mark the "I" (for "incorrect") space by every word which you misspelled. Do that now, before reading on.

Next look at every word marked "I" to decide whether your misspelling of it was caused by carelessness—for example, by an accidental failure to dot an *i* or to cross a *t*. Put a mark in the "C" (for "careless") space by each word which you carelessly misspelled. Do it now, before reading on.

TABULATING THE RESULTS

Now, following the instructions given on pages 152-155, fill out the profile on page 170 and the tabulation of totals on page 172. Do that now, before reading on.

COMPARING THE DIAGNOSTIC AND FINAL TESTS

How much progress you have made in improving your spelling by your work with this book will be revealed by a comparison of the profiles and tabulations of totals filled out for the two tests, taken before and after your work with the book. Especially important is a comparison of your sense of doubt before and after this work, for a healthy sense of doubt and conscientious proofreading will, more than anything else, enable you to continue to improve your spelling in the future.

THE PROFILE

Item Number								Name of Problem	Chapter Number	Total Missed	Total Doubted
Part one											
1	14	27	40	53	66	79	92	Unstressed vowels	5		
2	15	28	41	54	67	80	93	Omitted and added letters	6, 7		
3	16	29	42	55	68	81	94	Identical pronunciations	8		
4	17	30	43	56	69	82	95	Similar pronunciations	9		
5	18	31	44	57	70	83	96	IE or EI	10		
6	19	32	45	58	71	84	97	Final doubling	11		
7	20	33	46	59	72	85	98	Final E	12		
8	21	34	47	60	73	86	99	Assimilative doubling	13		
9	22	35	48	61	74	87	100	Additive doubling	14		
10	23	36	49	62	75	88	101	Final Y	15		
11	24	37	50	63	76	89	102	Other final letters	16		
12	25	38	51	64	77	90	103	Internal doubling	17		
13	26	39	52	65	78	91	104	Competing spellings	18		
Part two											
1	2	3	4	5	6	7	8	Compound words	19		

ANSWERS, FINAL TEST

PART ONE

1. despises	36. magnifies	70. forfeit
2. accuracy	37. elves	71. traveled
3. immigrants	38. parallel	72. truly
4. advice	39. favor	73. immoral
5. freight	40. maintenance	74. socially
6. fanned	41. government	75. lovelies
7. dining	42. complement	76. halos
8. support	43. devised	77. vaccinated
9. misspent	44. grieve	78. fibers
10. tying	45. transferred	79. defiant
11. melodies	46. manageable	80. soften
12. terrible	47. oppress	81. fourth
13. abridgment	48. evilly	82. stature
14. discover	49. medleys	83. shield
15. luxury	50. trafficking	84. deferred
16. stationary	51. fallacy	85. gravely
17. bath	52. meter	86. original
18. variety	53. propaganda	87. dissatisfied
19. thinning	54. condemn	88. jockeys
20. firing	55. altogether	89. mottoes
21. corrupt	56. precede	90. difference
22. unnatural	57. piece	91. through
23. signifies	58. concurred	92. sponsor
24. cameos	59. duly	93. pumpkin
25. difficult	60. irrational	94. there
26. though	61. cruelly	95. proceeded
27. diminish	62. carries	96. deceive
28. family	63. commandos	97. quizzed
29. counsel	64. horrors	98. judgment
30. absorb	65. clamor	99. immature
31. deity	66. comparative	100. override
32. biggest	67. surprise	101. necessities
33. traceable	68. imminent	102. cargoes
34. appeal	69. supersedes	103. tyranny
35. dissimilar		104. dialogue

PART TWO

1. B	3. A	5. C	7. A
2. A	4. C	6. C	8. C

THE TABULATION OF TOTALS

1. Total number of words lined or marked "I" (for "incorrect") _____

2. Total circled or marked "D" (for "doubtful") _____

3. Total marked "I" and "D," thus: _____

D   I   C   or   (53)
✓   ✓   ___

4. Total marked "I," but not "D"
Subtract the number in line 3, above, from that in line 1, above. _____

5. Total marked "D," but not "I"
Subtract the number in line 3 from that in line 2. _____

6. Total marked "C" (for "careless")
Count the number marked "C" on your test sheets. _____

7. Total marked "I," but not "D" or "C"
Add the numbers in line 3 and 6. Then subtract that total from the number in line 1. Enter the result here: _____

8. Total marked "I" and "D" or "C"
Subtract the number in line 7 from that in line 1. _____

For an interpretation of the tabulation of totals, see pages 157-161.

COMMON PREFIXES
AND SUFFIXES

PREFIXES

Below are some prefixes most frequently used in English, their customary meanings, and examples of their combinations with stems:

Prefix	Meaning	Combination	Meaning
ab	away, from	absent abduct	sent from lead away
ad	to, toward	adhere advent	stick to coming to
ante	before	antecedent	coming before
anti	against	antifreeze	against freezing
com	with, together	complaint combine	with discontent bind together
de	down	descent	go down
dis	apart, not	distend disease	stretch apart not with ease
ex	out	export	carry out
in[1]	in	include	close in
in[2]	not	infirm insane	not strong not sane
inter	among, between	international interchange	among nations change between
mis	wrong	misspelling	wrong spelling

Prefix	Meaning	Combination	Meaning
per	through	perchance	through chance
pre	before	predict	say before
		prehistoric	before history
pro	forward	progress	move forward
		project	throw forward
re	again, back	repeat	say again
		reverse	turn back
sub	under	submarine	under the sea
super	over	supervise	look over
trans	across	transport	carry across

Running your eyes down the second column in that tabulation, you will discover that most of those prefixes have the meaning of prepositions: *from, to, before, against, with,* and so on. Thus it is no accident that the words *prefix,* meaning "to fasten in front of," and *preposition,* meaning "to place before," begin in exactly the same way, with *pre.* A prefix is a part of a word, while a preposition is a word, a part of speech, and therefore a part of a sentence; but the two are often alike in conveying the same sort of meaning.

SUFFIXES

As a rule, suffixes do not convey a meaning, as prefixes do. Instead, they usually perform a grammatical function: they change one part of speech into another—say, an adjective into a noun, as when *good* becomes *goodness.* They most often carry out one of four such functions, which may be described by four words: they "nominalize" when converting something into a noun, "verbalize" when converting it into a verb, "adjectivalize" when converting it into an adjective, and "adverbalize" when converting it into an adverb. That is why "function" rather than "meaning" is included in the following tabulation of some of the suffixes which occur most frequently:

Suffix	Function	Example
able	adjectivalize	change / changeable
acy	nominalize	literate / literacy*
al	adjectivalize	occasion / occasional
ance	nominalize	abundant / abundance*
ancy	nominalize	constant / constancy*
ar	nominalize	lie / liar*
ence	nominalize	evident / evidence*
ency	nominalize	despondent / despondency*
ent	nominalize	correspond / correspondent
er	nominalize	dive / diver*
ful	adjectivalize	hope / hopeful
hood	nominalize	likely / likelihood*
ible	adjectivalize	reduce / reducible*
ical	adjectivalize	philosophy / philosophical*
ify	verbalize	pure / purify*
ion	nominalize	possess / possession
ish	adjectivalize	style / stylish*
ism	nominalize	capital / capitalism
ity	nominalize	pure / purity*
ize	verbalize	satire / satirize*
less	adjectivalize	care / careless
like	adjectivalize	home / homelike
ly	adverbalize	pure / purely
ment	nominalize	govern / government
ness	nominalize	soft / softness
or	nominalize	supervise / supervisor*
sion	nominalize	erode / erosion*
ty	nominalize	novel / novelty
ward	adverbalize	home / homeward
wise	adverbalize	side / sidewise

*Notice how the spelling is changed when these two word-parts are combined. Such changes are discussed in Chapters 11-16.

F

LIST OF
FREQUENT
MISSPELLINGS

Every word in the following alphabetized list has been found in at least one list of words most frequently misspelled by students in high school and especially in college. Most words here were recorded in several of those lists.

Each word was misspelled because of one or more trouble spots in it, and each trouble spot is discussed in one or more chapters of this book. After each word in this list, therefore, are numbers designating the chapters dealing with the trouble spot(s) in the word—an indication of where you can get help in learning to spell it and other words like it.

Whenever you learn that you have misspelled a word—for example, a teacher has marked a misspelling in a paper of yours—write that word in your personalized list of misspellings (Chapter 4) and also look it up in this list. Often (but not always) you will find it here, accompanied by the number(s) of the chapter(s) dealing with its trouble spot(s). Put the number(s) next to the word in your personalized list. When a number begins to appear repeatedly there, study or review the chapter designated by the number. In general, the more often a number appears in that list, the greater your need to study or review the designated chapter.

Only one form of a word has, as a rule, been included in this composite list, though the underlying lists may have included more than one form. For example, only the form *acceptance* is in this list, but the underlying lists may have included such other forms as *accept, accepts, accepted, accepting, acceptable, acceptably, acceptability,* and *acceptableness*. If you misspell any form of a word listed here, consult the chapter(s) designated for the one form listed here. Indeed, some of the designated chapters are appropriate only for forms not included here.

absence, 9, 18
absorption, 9
acceptance, 5, 13
accidentally, 5, 13, 14

accommodate, 5, 13, 17
accompanies, 13, 15
accomplish, 5, 13
accustom, 5, 13

G
PERSONALIZED LIST OF MISSPELLINGS

For instructions about the preparation of this list, see pages 30-31.